GREAT
PERSONAL
POWER

THE SCIENCE OF SUCCESS

JOHN WEST

Great Personal Power

DEDICATED

Andrew Carnegie, who inspired organizing the world's first practical philosophy of American achievement, which makes the know-how of success available to the humblest person.

Mr. Carnegie believed if these principles were properly taught in public schools across the country it would revolutionize the entire educational system and reduce time spent in school to less than half.

Henry Ford, whose astounding achievements form the Foundation for practically all the principles of the Philosophy.

Dr. Napoleon Hill who began at an early age to study great achievers such as Andrew Carnegie, Thomas Edison, and Alexander Graham Bell, and received valuable assistance in person from some of the greatest men our country ever produced.

Dr. Napoleon Hill became the world's foremost scholar and thinker in the science of human success.

CONTENTS

PREFACE

"Great Personal Power" is destined to become one of the most influential books of all time in pointing the way to personal achievement, to financial independence, and to riches of the spirit beyond measurement in money.

The philosophy was inspired by Andrew Carnegie, the multimillionaire who disclosed his "Secret (formula)" of personal achievement to Napoleon Hill, the author of the book Think and Grow Rich.

Mr. Carnegie not only made himself a multimillionaire, but made millionaires of more than a score of men and women with whom he had shared his secret to success. Thousands of successful people have applied these principles for their own enrichment. The secrets, which lead to success, are made available to those who greatly desire to make money and attain the rich spiritual satisfaction that achievement can bring into one's life.

"Great Personal Power" is preeminently a "what to do and a how to do it" book. In it you will find a definite major purpose, a pleasing personality, the mastermind, applied faith, personal initiative, and a wealth of other principles to help you achieve your every goal and dream.

The principles of the philosophy of Great Personal Power will prepare you to attract and enjoy the higher brackets of success, which have always been and always will be denied to all except those who are ready for them.

The "Great Riches" within your own grasp cannot always be measured in money. There are riches in lasting friendships, sympathy and understanding between business associates, and in harmonious family relationships and inner harmony, which bring peace of mind measurable only in spiritual values.

Be prepared for a changed life when you begin to put into action the principles of Great Personal Power will not only ease the trials and stresses of everyday living, but also prepare you for the accumulation of material riches in abundance.

—*The Publisher*

A WORD FROM THE AUTHOR

In the power-packed pages of this book, you will find the "Carnegie Money-making Secret Formula" which has made fortunes for hundreds of exceedingly wealthy men and women all over the world.

The "Secret Formula" was brought to my attention while reading Napoleon Hill's book, Think and Grow Rich. When I first grasped the "Carnegie Secret Formula", I decided to spend the last fourteen years of my life studying Dr. Napoleon Hill's books and listening to his lectures.

So, one day I would share my work with others around the world, to men and women who, without the "Secret Formula," might go through life as failures.

Through the power-packed pages of this book, you will find the "Carnegie Money-making Secret Formula" which will work for everyone who is ready for it. The "money-making secret formula" is now being passed around the entire country for everyone's own personal benefit, as I planned that it should be passed around the country and all other countries.

Many people are using it to make a fortune while others are using it successfully in creating harmony in the workplace and in their homes.

In one chapter you will find the story of Arthur Nash, a Cincinnati tailor, who used his near-bankrupt business as a guinea pig on which to test the "secret formula". That business came to life and made a fortune for its owner and the employees of that clothing company.

The "Carnegie Secret Formula" to which I am referring is in every chapter of this book, but it is not directly named, for it seems to work more successfully when it is uncovered and left in sight, where those who are ready, and searching for it, may pick it up and put it in to use.

If you are ready for the "secret formula," you will recognize it after you finish reading the pages of this book.

I wish I might feel privileged to tell you how you will know if you are ready, but that would deprive you of much of the personal benefit you will receive when you make the discovery in your own way.

Have you ever been discouraged or had many difficulties to surmount which took the very soul out of you? Maybe, you have tried and failed, or maybe been handicapped by some illness or physical affliction.

The story of my discovery and use of the "money-making secret formula" may prove to be the missing link of the lost hope for which you have been searching in life. There is a peculiar thing about the "Carnegie Money-making Secret Formula".

Those who acquire and use it find themselves literally swept on to success. If you doubt what I just stated is not true, study the names of the people around the country who have used it, and check their records for yourself, and be convinced.

There is one definite thing I have discovered. There is no such thing as something for nothing. The "secret formula" to which I am referring cannot be had without a price, although its price is far less than its value. Those who are not intentionally searching for the "secret formula" cannot have it at any price, because it cannot be given away or be purchased for money, for it comes in two parts.

The first part is already in your possession if you have the courage to put it to use. Education has nothing to do with it, because long before I was born, the "money-making secret formula" found its way into the possession of Thomas A. Edison. Mr. Edison used it so intelligently that he became the world's leading inventor, with only three months of formal schooling.

That should convince you that "Great Riches" are not beyond your reach and you can still be what you wish to be with all the money, fame, recognition, and happiness you so desire.

How do I know all of these things?

You will find that answer when you finish reading this book, or you might find it in the first chapter.

What is "education," anyway?

The answer to that question is in full detail throughout the entire book. Remember, too, while reading this book, it deals with facts, not with fiction. Its definite major purpose is to convey the great universal truth through which all who are ready may learn what to do and how to do it with the needed stimulus to make a start.

As a final word of preparation before you begin to read this book, all throughout the philosophy, reference is going to be made about the seven basic motives. These are the alphabet of success, and the emotions and desires that inspire all voluntary actions of people. They are the foundation on which this philosophy is built, for they are the basic building blocks of human character. They are vital to your understanding of other people, and the understanding of yourself, for they are a part of us all.

They are:

1. Emotion of Sex
2. Desire for Material Gain
3. Desire for Self-Preservation
4. Desire for Self-expression and Recognition
5. Desire for Life After Death
6. Desire for Revenge

7. Emotion of Fear

These motives mirror human nature. Some of them are positive; some of them are negative. These are the forces that motivate everybody and must be understood and worked with if you want to achieve The Great Riches of Life.

It is my intention to present this philosophy in the plainest and simplest terms available, so young men and women of grade-school age can understand and achieve what they desire in life.

—*John West*

1

A DEFINITE MAJOR PURPOSE

First Premise

The starting point of all individual achievement is the adoption of a definite major purpose accompanied by a definite plan for its attainment, followed by appropriate action.

It is not too important you start out with a plan that is 100 percent sound. In fact, it is not too important, because if you find out you have adopted a plan that is not 100 percent sound, and if it is not working, you can always change or modify that plan. It is very important that you are definite about your definite major purpose.

Second Premise

All individual achievements are the result of a motive or a combination of the seven basic motives. The seven basic motives described above are the forces that motivate all of us and must be understood, learned, and worked with if you really want to achieve the "Great riches of life".

Third Premise

All dominating ideas, plans, or purposes held in the mind of any individual through repetition of thought and emotionalized with a burning desire for its realization; are taken over by the subconscious mind and acted upon through whatever natural or logical means that may be available.

If you have the mind to pick up an idea, the mind will automatically act upon that idea and form a habit. You must tell the mind what it is you want repeatedly with no end to the repetition.

Fourth Premise

All dominating desires, plans, or purpose backed up with the state of mind known as faith, and emotionalized with a burning desire for its realization is automatically sensed by the subconscious section of the mind and acted upon immediately.

When I say all dominating desires, plans, or purpose backed up with the state of mind known as faith, I do not refer to wishing or hoping or mildly believing in things. I mean a positive state of mind known as faith where you can see your definite major purpose already in its finished act even before you begin. That's pretty positive, isn't it?

I have never failed at anything I ever started out to do, unless I got careless in my desire to do it, backed away from it, or changed my mind or my positive mental attitude.

I want you to know you can put yourself in a positive state of mind known as faith to achieve anything you start out to do in life, unless, you weaken as you go along, as so many people do through life.

Do you know the percentage of our brothers and sisters around the country who sell themselves short throughout life, because they do not have the right amount of confidence, let alone the right amount of positive faith in themselves? Give a guess to the percentage? It is somewhere between 98 and 100 percent. Isn't it strange how Mother Nature works?

She gives each and every one of us a set of tools adequate for our every need to aspire for and to have in this world.

Then she rewards each and every one of us bountifully for just accepting those tools and using them. She penalizes a man or woman beyond compare if they do not accept those tools and use them.

Mother Nature hates vacuums and idleness. It is because she wants everything to be in action. She especially wants the human mind to be active. The mind is no different than any other part of the physical body. If you do not use the mind or rely on it, the mind will atrophy, wither away, and become weak through disuse. Then you will not have the will power to even resist or protest when people push you around your whole life.

What Genius Lies Asleep in Your Brain?

Somewhere inside that great intelligent brain of

yours lies sleeping a genius, especially if your brain is aroused and put into action. That genius will carry you to heights you have never dreamed of before.

If you have observed, the most outstanding successful rich individuals in the world are people who found ways and means of appropriating most of their intelligence through their brain and putting it into action. Knowledge will not attract money, unless it is organized and intelligently directed through practical plans of action. Lack of understanding of this fact has been the source of confusion to millions of people all over the world who falsely believe that knowledge is power.

Knowledge becomes power only if it is organized into definite practical plans of action and directed to a definite end. The "missing link" in all systems of education is the failure of educational institutions to teach this fact to students, teach them how to organize their knowledge, and then use it after it is acquired.

The responsibility of this philosophy is to mainly give you a pattern or a blueprint by which you can take full control of your mind and organize your mind for riches. All you need do is follow the blueprint of this book.

The Major Benefits of a Definite Major Purpose

Having a definite major purpose automatically develops self-reliance, personal initiative, imagination, enthusiasm, self-discipline, and concentration of effort. All these are the main ingredients for achieving permanent success in any walk of life.

There is quite an array of things you can develop which have a definite major purpose. That is the equivalent of saying you know exactly what you want, and you have a plan to get what you desire most in your life. Then keep your mind occupied with the carrying out of that plan.

Unless you are a very unusual person, you will probably adopt some plans that do not work well in your life.

If you find that the plan you have adopted is not working and is not right, you should immediately discard that plan and get another until you do find one that does work for your life.

When I first organized this philosophy into a book, the original title was "Read and Grow Rich". I got it organized and sent it to the Napoleon Hill Foundation. I sent it to them with hope they could help me get it published.

Nothing happened, and many months passed. By this time, I lost my wife, my son, my house, my vending company and everything. I was crushed, heartbroken. I was losing everything, because I placed all my time, energy, and concentration on getting this philosophy organized into a book.

As soon as I lost everything, the first thing that

came to my mind was to call my mom and tell her what was happening in my life. My mom asked me what she could do to help to me.

I was not sure what to say, because I was an emotional wreck. Then the thought came to me that she could just give the Napoleon Hill Foundation a call and see what is holding things up.

My mom called the Napoleon Hill Foundation for me and was informed they are a non-profit organization. My mind went into shock. I just had spent over a year going through a home study self-improvement course called "Your Right to Be Rich", a series of lectures by Dr. Napoleon Hill, the world's greatest millionaire maker. I organized his course into a book and titled it "Read and Grow Rich". I was pretty sure I was the first person to ever do that in the history of the world. I was pretty sure I was going to be rich, and I believed I had a right to be rich.

All I needed to do was to get it into the hands of the Napoleon Hill Foundation, and they would handle the rest.

My plan failed, and I became as broke as a church mouse.

Instead of giving up and quitting, I came up with another plan. I would take matters into my own hands and get it published myself.

I borrowed some money from my mom. I reassembled some things from the original book I sent to the Napoleon Hill Foundation. I used the same title, "Read and Grow Rich". Not long after, I got "Read and Grow Rich" published.

I got a letter from the Napoleon Hill Foundation, and the title was copyrighted.

My first thought was incredulity. How could the title be copyrighted when it never existed before? I checked.

I suspected from the time I got the idea and had it sent to them, someone else got the idea and used it before me.

At this time in my life I was pretty much ready to just give up and quit.

Then I got excited. I got excited, because I was thinking maybe I can be an inspiration to millions of other people who go through defeat and failure, and then eventually give up. I made the decision to keep working on this book no matter how hard or tough things got for me. All I really needed to do was just come up with another million-dollar box office title and rewrite the book. I have spent many years rewriting this book. I have spent many years trying to come up with a different million-dollar box office title to use. None of them had been any good.

Then something great happened to me one morning. I finally came up with a million-dollar box office title for this book and would like to share how I did it. This story that I am about to share is ladened with food for thought, my friend.

I knelt by on the side of my bed one night to have a nice little talk with my subconscious mind. I said, "Now look here, old sub. You and I have gone a long way together in life. We've really done some good things together, and we've really done some dumb things together, thanks to my ignorance. I have got to come up with a million-dollar box office title, and I want it by tomorrow morning. Do you understand that?"

I climbed into my bed to sleep. Then I woke up very early the next morning feeling as if somebody shook me to wake me up. As I came out of my sleep, *Great Personal Power* was in my mind. Oh, boy! I jumped out of my bed, did a cartwheel, and ran to the table to write the title down.

I grabbed the telephone and called my son. I woke him up.

He answered, "What's the matter, Dad? Did I forget to set my alarm, and I'm late for work?"

"You bet you are with a million-dollar box office title."

"A million-dollar box office title? What is it?"

"Great Personal Power."

"Boy, Dad, you've got it!"

I'll say we finally got it. This book will gross over a million dollars, and I'm hoping for a billion dollars before I pass on. A million-dollar title, a multimillion dollar title. If you want results from prayer, you must condition your mind, so your life is a prayer. You must condition your mind from day to day, so when any emergency arises or pops up, you can deal with it.

Having a definite major purpose induces one to budget one's time and income, and helps one plan all day-to-day endeavors, which lead to the attainment of one's definite major purpose.

Have you ever sat down for a minute in your busy schedule to kept track of the amount of time you waste each day for one week? Then, that is the amount of time you could devote to educate yourself if you wanted to educate yourself badly enough.

We are not efficient; we have eight hours to sleep, another eight hours to earn a living, and another eight hours of free time here in this great country where we live. Having a definite major purpose makes one more alert in recognizing opportunities related to the object of one's definite major purpose.

It also inspires the necessary courage to act and embrace those opportunities when they appear in our life. We all see opportunities almost every day of our lives which, if we would act and embrace them, could benefit all of us. However, there is something in all of us called procrastination. We just do not have the will power or the alertness or the determination to embrace opportunities when they come along. If you will condition your mind with this philosophy. You will not only embrace opportunities, you can do something better than embrace an opportunity. What could you do better? Make the opportunity, that's the idea!

One of George Washington's soldiers came to him one day when they were preparing an attack on the next morning.

This soldier said, "Sir, the conditions and the circumstances are not quite right for the attack tomorrow morning," to which Washington replied, "The circumstances and conditions are not right for the attack tomorrow morning? Well, I make conditions and circumstances. Attack!"

I have never seen a successful man or woman in any business who responds, "Attack!" when somebody says, "It can't be done." Start where you are, and when you get to the curve in the road, you cannot see past till you get there.

You will find that road always goes on around that curve.

Don't procrastinate and don't stand still. Attack!

Having a **definite major purpose** inspires confidence in one's integrity and character, and it attracts the favorable attention of other people.

I think the whole world loves to see a man or a woman walking with their chest sticking out, walking in an atmosphere that tells the whole world they know exactly what they are doing. You know people will get out of the way on the sidewalk, and let you go by them if you are determined to get by them. You don't have to whistle or holler at them.

You just need to send your thoughts ahead with the determination that you are going through that crowd. The world is like that, because when a man or women knows where they are going, they will always find willing helpers to cooperate with them. That's the greatest benefit of having a definite major purpose.

It opens the way for the full exercise of that state of mind known as applied faith. It makes your mind positive and frees your mind up from the limitations of fear, doubt, discouragement, indecision, and procrastination.

The minute you decide upon a definite major purpose, and you know you're going to achieve it, all the negative thoughts you had in the past just pick up their baggage and move out of your mind. Negative thoughts cannot live in a positive mind.

Can you imagine a negative thought and a positive one occupying the same space at the same time? No, you can't, because it can't be done. Did you know the slightest bit of negative mental attitude is enough to destroy the power of prayer? Did you know that the slightest bit of negative mental attitude is enough to destroy your plan for carrying out your definite major purpose?

You must move with courage, applied faith, and

determination to carry out your definite major purpose.

Stumbled on the book Think and Grow Rich. But, I had a silent person looking over my shoulder telling me to spit it out, tell yourself you can do it. I said to myself, "I will complete this book and help make the world a better place."

My mind was on fire with the belief I could write a book even though I didn't have the slightest asset to give me a beginning other than my determination. I would get the necessary assets to complete this book in my lifetime. Napoleon Hill's books and lectures brought out something in my mind that I have been searching for years.

I did not know its value. I found out the value of it later.

I want you to recognize the value of it, because you have the same thing in your mind. That same capacity to know what you want and to become self-determined will get you what you want, even though you may not know where to make the first start in life.

What does make a great man or a great woman? Greatness is the ability to recognize the power of your own mind, and start using that great mind. In my book of rules, every man and every woman can become truly great by the simple process of recognizing the power of his or her own mind and using that great mind.

Here are the instructions for applying a definite major purpose. These instructions should be carried out to the letter:

> 1. Write out a complete clear statement of your definite major purpose, sign it, and commit it to memory.
>
> 2. Then repeat your definite major purpose once a day in the form of a prayer, or an affirmation if you choose.

You can see the advantage of this, because it places your faith in your Creator squarely behind you. I have found this from experience, or as I call it the "university of hard knocks", the weakest spot in a student's activity. They read that and say, "Well, that's simple enough. Why should I go through trouble of writing out my definite major purpose?"

You might just as well set this book down and never pick it up again if you're going to take that kind of negative mental attitude. You must write out your definite major purpose and go through the physical act of translating a thought onto paper.

Then start talking to your subconscious mind about your definite major purpose.

It will not do you a bit of harm if you remember the story I told you of what I did to get my million-dollar box office title. It will not do a bit of harm for you to get your subconscious mind to understand from here on you are going to become the boss, and you are going to take charge starting today.

You cannot expect the subconscious mind or any-body else to help you find your definite major purpose if you do not know what you want in life. Ninety-eight out of one hundred people, taking a cross-section of humanity in general, do not know what they want in their life.

Consequently, 98% of people never get what they want but take whatever life hands them. Let's make sure you are not one of them.

Here are some additions for your definite major purpose

In addition to your definite major purpose, you can have as many minor purposes as you want, provided they are related, and they lead you in the direction of your overall lifelong definite major purpose. Your whole life should be devoted to carrying out your definite major purpose.

Find out what you want in your life, and incidental-ly, it is alright to be humble like I am when you go to ask for what you want in your life. But don't be too humble.

Reach out and ask for the king's ransom and what-ever you consider to be your definite major overall purpose. Write it out clearly and set the time limits.

For example, "I intend to attain within so-and-so years so-and-so." Then describe what the "so-and-so" is going to be in your plan. In the paragraph below that one, write down what you intend to give in return for that so-and-so you requested. Continue by describing what you intend to give in return for that so-and-so in your plan.

Now, as to timing, did you know nature has a system of timing everything we plan? For example, you are a farmer, and plant some wheat in the field. You must first prepare the ground and examine the soil to make sure it has the right elements to plant the seed. Then you must plant the seed at the right season of the year and at the right depth in the ground. Then what do you do?

Do you go back the very next day with a harvester and start harvesting? No, you will have to time everything properly and wait for nature to do her part.

Whether Mother Nature or God or Infinite Intelligence or whatever you choose to call that first cause, we are still talking about same thing. There is an intelligence that does its part if you do your part first. Infinite Intelligence will not direct you to your definite major purpose or attract to you the object of your definite major purpose.

Unless you do know what your definite major purpose is going to be in life, you will have to properly time it right.

It would be ridiculous if you started out with only a mediocre talent and say you are going to make a million dollars in the next thirty days because talents are developed. Make your definite major purpose within reason of what you know you can achieve. You will want to keep your plan for your definite major purpose flexible.

Do not become too assured that the plan you worked out is perfect just because you worked it out. Leave your plan flexible and give it a good trial. If it is not working properly, change your plan. Call your definite major purpose into your consciousness as often as it may be practical.

Eat with it, sleep with it, and take it with you wherever you go, keeping in mind the fact your subconscious mind can thus be influenced to work for its attainment while you sleep. Each night just before you go to bed, give your subconscious mind some sort of list of what you want done the next day. Make sure the healing of the body is on the list, because the body needs repairing every day.

When you lay the body down to sleep each night, turn it over to infinite intelligence, and request for your subconscious mind to go to work and heal every cell and every organ, giving you the next morning a perfectly conditioned body from which the mind may function.

Do not go to bed without giving orders to your subconscious mind. Get into the habit of telling your subconscious mind what you want in your life. If you keep on long enough, it will believe you and deliver to you what you order, so you better be careful about what you order. If you keep on asking for it, you are going to get it. I wonder if you would not be surprised if you knew what you have been asking for through the years. You have been asking for it, because everything you have right now that you did not want, you have been asking for it.

Maybe through neglect and maybe you did not tell the subconscious mind what you really wanted, but it stocked up on a lot of stuff you did not want, and that is just the way it is with your mind.

Here are the major important factors for your definite major purpose in life

A man or woman's definite major purpose should represent their greatest single purpose above all others they desire to achieve, and the fruits of which they are willing to leave behind as a monument to themselves.

If you do not have a definite major overall purpose, you are just wasting the better portion of your life. The wear and tear of living is not worth the price you must pay unless you are going somewhere with this opportunity here on this planet.

I imagine you were sent over here to do something with a mind capable of hewing out and attaining your own destiny. If you do not attain that destiny and use that great mind, I imagine your life to a large extent will have been wasted from the viewpoint of the one who sent you over.

Do not believe because in the past you have not achieved as much as hoped, that you cannot achieve in the future.

Do not measure your future by your past. If you do, you are sunk.

A new day is coming. You are setting up a new pattern. You are in a new world. You are a new person. If not, why not?

I intend that everyone reading this book will grow mentally, physically, and maybe spiritually, with a new aim in life, a new purpose, a new realization of your own *Great Personal Power* and your own dignity as a human being.

If you were to ask me what I believe to be the greatest sin of mankind, you would be surprised at what my answer would be. What would yours be on that subject? The greatest sin of mankind is neglecting to use his greatest asset _ his mind.

It is bound to be, because if a man uses that greatest asset, he would have everything in his life in abundance. Having a definite major purpose, or a portion of one's definite major purpose should remain a few jumps ahead of them always as something to look forward to with hope and anticipation.

If you ever do catch up with your definite major purpose and attain your definite major purpose, then what?

You should get another one, and you will have

learned after attaining your first one that you can attain a definite major purpose or minor purpose.

Then, chances are you will make your next definite major purpose bigger, and then the next year double that one.

Life is less interesting when one has no definite major purpose to be attained or achieved other than merely living.

The hope of future achievement coupled with a definite major purpose is among man's greatest pleasures.

Sorry indeed is a man caught up with himself and has nothing more to do in life. I have found a lot of them and most of them are miserable. No, you must keep active, and you must keep an objective ahead of you in life.

Having a definite major purpose should be so designed to consume an entire lifetime of endeavor. It should harmonize with one's business, occupation, or profession.

Each day's work should enable one to come one day closer to the attainment of their definite major purpose.

I cannot imagine anybody reading this book satisfying him or herself with just an existence. I think you want to live in abundance. I think you want everything that is necessary for you to do the things you want to do, including money.

Having a definite major purpose may consist of having many different combinations of lesser aims, such as the nature of one's occupation, which should be something of one's own choice.

When you start to write out your definite major purpose, write it out like planks in a platform, "#1 so-and-so," "#2 so-and-so," and somewhere at the top near the head be sure to include "perfect harmony" between yourself and your mate. Do you think that is important? Do know anything more important than a man and his wife? Have you ever seen or heard of a relationship of a man and his wife where there was not harmony?

It is not pleasant to be around people who are not in step with each other. You can be harmonious, and here is where you should start applying your master-mind relationship first. Your wife or your husband should be your first mastermind ally.

You might have to go back and court them all over again. I cannot think of anything I have ever done in my whole life I enjoyed as much as courting. If you are not on right terms with your business associates or your fellow workers, those people you work with each day, go back and rededicate yourself to the business of striking off on a new basis. Acknowledge that maybe you are not entirely the most perfect person in the whole world. Maybe the other person will say, "Come to think about it, neither am I," and then you are off to the car races.

The human relationship plank is most important for one's definite major purpose, because that purpose can only be achieved through the cooperation of other people. Have you ever realized that for great things to be accomplished it must be done through the harmonious cooperation of other people?

How can we expect to get harmonious cooperation with other people if we do not understand the seven basic motives and understand each other? The universal application of the principle of a definite major purpose may be seen by observing how nature applies a definite major purpose. If there is anything in the universe that is definite, it is the laws of nature. They do not deviate, and they do not temporize. They do not subside, and you cannot go around them or avoid them. You can learn their nature, adjust yourself to them, and benefit from them.

Nobody has ever heard of the law of gravitation being suspended, not even for a fraction of a second. It never has been done, and it never will be done. Nature's setup throughout the whole universe, system of universes perhaps, is so definite that everything moves with precision like clockwork.

If you want to see an example of the necessity of an individual moving with a definite major purpose, you need only to have a smattering of understanding of the natural sciences to see the way nature does things: the orderliness of the universe, the interrelation of the entire natural laws, the fixation of all the stars and planets in an immovable relationship to one another.

Isn't it a great thing to know the astronomers can sit down with a pencil and a few pieces of paper and predetermine hundreds of years in advance the exact relationship of given planets and stars where they will be in relationship to one another. They could not do that if there was not a purpose or a plan under which they are working. We want to find out what that purpose is as it relates to us as individuals.

This is the little bit I have picked up from life and from the life experiences of other men and women. So, you may learn how to adjust yourself to the laws of nature, so you may benefit by these laws instead of allowing yourself to be abused by your neglecting to use them.

To me, one of the most horrible things to contemplate is the possible cessation of all the natural laws. Imagine the chaos of all the stars and planets running together. Why, they would make the H-bomb look like a small firecracker if nature allowed her laws to be suspended. She does not do that because she has very definite laws to go by.

You will find out when you check these seventeen principles they check perfectly with all the laws of nature.

When you to the chapter on going the extra mile, you will find Mother Nature is profound in her application of the principle of going the extra mile.

When Mother Nature produces blooms on trees, she does not just produce enough to fill the trees. She produces enough to take care of the damage from the winds and the storms. When she produces fish in the sea, she does not produce just enough to perpetuate more fish. She produces enough to feed the bullfrogs, the snakes, the alligators, and all the other things, and still has enough left over to carry out her purpose.

She also forces a man to go the extra mile, or else he would perish in one season. If a man did not go the extra mile, and Nature did not compensate him when he goes out to put a grain of wheat in the ground by giving him back five hundred to a thousand grains to compensate him for his intelligence, we would starve to death in one season. If you will do your part, Mother Nature will do her part, and she will do it in superabundance.

One of the strange things about nature occurs when you keep your mind focused on the positive side. It becomes greater than the negative side. If you will keep your mind focused on the positive side, it will become greater than all the negative thoughts that may try to penetrate your mind and influence your life.

Start looking around, and you will find living examples of people you want to emulate and people you do not want to emulate. You might see people who are failing and be able to tell why these people are failing. I dare say from this time on you will be able to use this philosophy as a measuring stick wherever you find a success or a failure.

You will be able to lay your finger right on the cause of it, and that includes you too in life.

> *I like to see a man proud of his country, and I like to see him so live that his country is proud of him.*
> —Lincoln

2

THE MASTERMIND

First Premise

The Mastermind principle is the medium through which one may procure the full benefits, the experience, the training, the education, the specialized knowledge, and influence of others, completely, as if their minds were really one's own.

Did you know that whatever it is you lack in education, knowledge, and influence, you can always attain from somebody who exhibits that in life? The exchange of favors and of knowledge are the greatest exchanges in the entire world. It is a great thing to engage in business where the exchange of money earns you a profit. I would much rather exchange ideas with a man or woman and give them an idea they did not have and receive an idea I did not have.

Then I would the exchange of money.

You may, of course, already know that Thomas A. Edison was perhaps the greatest inventor the world has ever known.

Mr. Edison was dealing with many sciences, and it

may surprise you to know that Mr. Edison knew nothing about the sciences. You would think it would be impossible for a man to succeed in any undertaking, unless they were educated in that field.

In my research I was astounded to find out Andrew Carnegie personally did not know anything about the making and the marketing of steel. His part or job was to keep the members of his mastermind alliance working in a spirit of perfect harmony. You are probably laughing and thinking, is that all he had to do?

Have you ever in your life tried to get any two people to agree on anything for three minutes in succession? If you have not tried to do that yet, you should try to do that someday. Getting other people to work together in a spirit of perfect harmony is one of the greatest of all human achievements.

Mr. Carnegie's mastermind group consisted of a metallurgist, a chemist, a plant works manager, a legal advisor, a chief of his financial staff, and so on down the line. There were over twenty individuals working together whose combined education, experience, and knowledge constituted all there was to know about the making and marketing of steel. It was not necessary for Mr. Carnegie to have that knowledge, because he had people all around him who did understand the making and the marketing of steel. It was his job to keep them working in a spirit of perfect harmony.

Second Premise

An active mastermind alliance of two or more minds working together in a spirit of perfect harmony for the attainment of a common objective stimulates each individual mind in that alliance to move with more courage than one ordinarily experiences, and it prepares the way for that state of mind known as applied faith.

Have you ever had an experience with an automobile when the battery runs down? You come outside some morning to start your car and turn on the key, but nothing happens?

Man's brain may be compared to an electric battery that periodically needs to be charged. A successful man needs to have a source for charging that battery and keeping it charged.

It is the same thing if a man wakes up feeling negative in the morning. If he selects a good mate, and she's a good coordinator and helps to charge his battery, chances are, when he comes back home that night, he will come back home with what he went out to achieve.

Third Premise

A mastermind alliance, properly conducted, stimulates each individual mind in the alliance to move with enthusiasm, personal initiative, imagination, and courage to a degree far above one experiences when moving without such an alliance.

In my early beginning, I had a mastermind alliance of three people. I had a mastermind alliance with Napoleon Hill through reading his books and listening to his lectures with my son. We three nourished this philosophy through the stages when everyone else was making fun of me for undertaking to serve the richest man in the world without any compensation.

There was a whole lot of logic to what they were saying, because I had not received any monetary compensation out of it. There finally came a time when the laughing was on the other side of the fence. That took plenty of pain and tears shed before I did get to the point where I could laugh back at those who laughed at me.

That wonderful relationship I established with Napoleon Hill through his books and his lectures, and with my son enabled me to offset what my friends and everyone else who knew what I was engaged in while writing this book.

There are times when you undertake anything above mediocrity that you are going to meet with opposition.

You are going to meet people who poke fun at you. Most of them will be close to you, and some of them perhaps your own relatives.

You will need to have some source to which you can turn when you are aiming above mediocrity. You will need some source to get your battery charged and keep it charged, so you do not quit when the going gets hard, and you will not pay any attention when someone criticizes you. I have become immune to all forms of criticism through the relationship I built up under my mastermind alliance. Had it not been for Napoleon Hill's books and lectures, and my son, you would not be reading this book, and it would not be spread out all over the world helping millions of people.

I had at least a million opportunities to give up and quit in my life. Every one of them looked very alluring. I can assure you of that fact. There were many times in my life when I felt I was the stupidest man alive if I did not quit.

But, I could always go back to Napoleon's books and listen to his lectures. I could call my son on the phone and have a nice little chat with him. My son would always tell me "Remember what you always tell me, Dad. 'A winner never quits, and a quitter never wins.'"

There were many times when I did not even have two pennies to rub together, as my enemies were saying.

My son would say, "Dad, you are going to become the richest man in the world. I can see it in the future." If you were to take all my riches and put all them together, I suspect I have more riches than all my relatives put together for three generations back on both sides of the family. My son could see what I was doing was bound to make me rich. I am not referring alone to monetary riches.

I am referring to those higher and broader riches you find when you can render service to many people all over the world.

Fourth Premise:

An effective mastermind alliance must be active.

You just cannot form an alliance with somebody and say, "Now that's it; we've got a mastermind alliance."

I am lined up with this person and that person and the other person. That amounts to absolutely nothing until each member of the mastermind alliance becomes active.

Each member of the alliance must step right in and start pitching in mentally, spiritually, financially, physically, and every way that is possible. Each member of the alliance must engage in the pursuit of a definite major purpose and move in a spirit of perfect harmony.

You do know the difference between a spirit of perfect harmony and ordinary harmony, right? I have had ordinary harmonious relationships with many people. A spirit of perfect harmony in any relationship is about the rarest thing in the entire world. I could count on the fingers of one hand of all the people with whom I have a relationship of a spirit of perfect harmony.

I have a very nice, polite, speaking acquaintance

with a lot of people, but that is not a spirit of perfect harmony.

A spirit of perfect harmony only exists when your relationship to the other person is such if they wanted everything you have, you will willingly turn it over to them.

That takes a lot of unselfishness to put yourself in that state of mind.

Mr. Carnegie stressed repeatedly to Napoleon Hill the importance of a relationship of a spirit of perfect harmony.

Mr. Carnegie said, "If you don't have a spirit of perfect harmony in a mastermind alliance, then it's not a mastermind alliance. It's just ordinary cooperation or friendly coordination of effort."

The mastermind alliance gives one full access to the spiritual powers of the other members of the alliance. It is not just the mental or the financial powers, but the spiritual powers. The feeling you get when you begin to establish permanency in your mastermind alliance is going to be one of the most outstanding and pleasant experiences in your entire life. When you are engaged in a mastermind activity, you will have an abundance of faith that no matter what you start out to do you will not have any doubts, any fears, or any limitations. That is a great confident state of mind to be in.

Fifth Premise

It is a matter of established record that all individual

successes based upon any kind of achievement above mediocrity is attained only through the mastermind principle, and not by individual effort alone.

Can you imagine how little you could accomplish if you did not have the cooperation of other people? Suppose you are in a profession, like a dentist, lawyer, doctor, osteopath, writer, speaker, or any profession. Then suppose you did not understand how to convert each one of your clients or patients into a salesman for yourself? Can you imagine how long it would take to build a following or sell your service?

The outstanding professionals do it by indirectly and make a salesman out of every person they serve. They do it by going the extra mile and by going out of their way to be of unusual service and make a salesman out of all their clients.

The most successes are the result of personal power, and personal power of enough proportions to enable one to rise above mediocrity which is not possible without the application of the mastermind principle.

During the first term of Franklin D. Roosevelt in the White House, Mr. Hill had the privilege of working with Mr. Roosevelt as a confidential advisor. It was Napoleon Hill who laid out the skeleton of the propaganda plan that took the words "business depression" out of the headlines of the newspapers, and substituted in their stead "business recovered."

You might not be old enough to remember what happened on that Black Sunday when they had a meeting down at the White House. So, I will share with you what happened.

All the banks were closed that following Monday morning, and there was a stampede all over this country. People were lined up in front of the banks all over the country to draw out their deposits. Everyone had lost confidence in their country, in their banks, and in themselves. I suppose they still had confidence in God.

But, most people did not show much confidence in God.

Something had to be done about the "business depression".

Mr. Hill sat down with Franklin D. Roosevelt and worked out a skeleton plan of procedure that created one of the most outstanding applications of the mastermind principle that this nation had ever seen.

It was only a matter of days until the salesmen on the road who had run out of funds were just laughing about it.

These salesmen were not in any way scared about the "business depression." Mr. Hill's own funds were closed, and this was funny.

When Mr. Hill found out what was going to happen, he got smart, ran down to the bank, and got a thousand-dollar bill. It was not even worth a nickel, because there was nobody who could make change for

John West

the thousand-dollar bill. Mr. Hill was not scared because everybody else was in the same boat as he was. Something had to be done about the "business depression ".

Franklin D. Roosevelt was a great leader who had great imagination and great courage. Mr. Roosevelt and Mr. Hill got both houses of Congress working together in a spirit of perfect harmony for the first time in the history of this nation. Both houses of Congress, Democrats and Republicans, got behind the president and forgot about what their political debates happened to be in life. There were no Democrats and no Republicans, just Americans backing the president with everything he needed to stop that stampede of fear.

The newspaper publishers of America published everything that was sent out and gave them marvelous space.

The radio station operators gave marvelous help, despite their political beliefs. All the churches, Catholics, Protestants, Jews, and Gentiles of this nation were pulling together as Americans. What a wonderful sight it was because every one of them got behind the president and made some sort of a contribution toward reestablishing faith in the people of this country.

During those hectic days, I am sure there was no doubt in the minds of the majority of people that Mr. Roosevelt was the finest man that could have possibly handled that chaotic condition.

Don't get me wrong. Politically, I am just speaking about a great man who did a great job during a time when it needed done, and he had a mastermind alliance that was unstoppable and unbeatable.

Let's Look at the Different Kinds of Mastermind Alliances You Can Have

There are different mastermind alliances for purely social or personal reasons consisting of one's relatives, friends, and religious advisors where no material gain is sought.

The most important type of a mastermind alliance is the one which may exist between a man and his wife.

If I were considered brilliant with great brain power or great magnetic powers, I want to emphasize the importance of a harmonious marriage. Go to work immediately and rededicate that marriage with a harmonious mastermind alliance based on this chapter.

It will bring joy, success, and health you never dreamed of.

It is a wonderful thing when a harmonious mastermind alliance exists between a man and his wife. You will be forming your first mastermind alliance for purely economic and financial advancement purposes. That is one of the reasons you are reading this book, and that is legitimate.

You should start immediately to form a mastermind alliance just for that purpose. Remember, there is no such thing as one person dominating. One person is the leader and coordinator and in no way should try to dominate any of their associates. Because the very moment you start to dominate anybody, you will find resistance and rebellion.

Despite the fact there might not be a spirit of perfect harmony but there is a motive for the Americans of free enterprise.

That motive becomes a motive for financial gain to inspire every individual to do his or her very best in life. Many industries and businesses today are beginning to understand instead of just having cooperation or coordination of effort between the management and workers.

Businesses can take a step further with the mastermind principle by sharing the management problems and by sharing the profits and everything. Wherever any business has adopted that policy the businesses have made more money. The employees all received more wages, and everybody is happy in life.

The general instructions for the forming and the maintenance of a mastermind alliance

Adopt a definite major purpose as an objective to be attained by the mastermind alliance choosing individual members whose education, experience, and influence are the greatest value in achieving the purpose.

How does one go about selecting the right partners for their mastermind alliance? The procedure should be the same as if you were starting into a business, even if the individual was brilliant and well educated. The reason being the more educated these people may be, the more dangerous they may be if they are not dependable.

If an individual was not loyal, I'd say the same thing. If an individual is not loyal to their friends, family and country, then to me they would have no character whatsoever, and I would want no part of them. I'm not interested in a man's or woman's ability until I have found out whether they are dependable and loyal.

What would come next in my book of rules?

A positive mental attitude because what good is a negative employee around you all the time?

You could pay them to stay away and keep ahead in the game.

What would come next?

Going the extra mile and applied faith.

Let me tell you something, my friend.

When you find a person that satisfies all those traits in your life, you've really found somebody, and you're in the presence of royalty.

In a business organization if you're only running a peanut stand or cool-aid stand, you might get by with one person.

If you're running a country or big organization, you might need a hundred persons. You can check very accurately and see these qualities are essential in a mastermind alliance relationship.

You couldn't have a spirit of perfect harmony unless you were working with somebody who checked 100 percent on all those six traits. Next, you will need to determine what benefit each member of the mastermind alliance will receive in return for their cooperation in the mastermind alliance.

Remember, normally nobody does things for nothing. Do you do things for nothing? What about when you give your love to someone, do you do that for nothing? Do you get anything in return? You get plenty out of love, even if the love you give is not returned. You can enjoy development and growth from the relationship.

No, the truth is there is no such thing as something for nothing. Nobody works without some form of compensation. There are many different forms of compensation, so you can't expect your mastermind allies to just jump in and help you make a fortune, unless, they are equally participating in the benefits that come out of that mastermind alliance.

There is the golden rule by which everyone must go abide in life. Everyone must benefit equally, whether it's a monetary benefit, a happiness benefit, or a peace of mind benefit, a social benefit, or whatever benefit happens to be in life. Never ask anyone to do anything without giving him or her adequate motive for getting it done.

If I went down to the bank to borrow a million dollars, what would be an adequate motive for the bank lending me that money? Two motives, both under the desire for financial gain. The bank would be delighted to loan me as much money as I could take away if I give them security or collateral. Then they're going to want a profit on that loan because that's what they're in business for, to make a profit.

There are other transactions not based upon the monetary motive. What is the motive when a man asks the girl of his choice to marry him, and then she accepts him?

Theoretically, it's love, but why does she accept him?

I want to share a personal story with you, my friend.

When my father started courting my mother before I was born, he used to work as a roofer in a roofing company.

My father had a tenth-grade education. My mother had a ninth-grade education at that time but eventually got a GED. I can still remember as a small boy seeing my mother teach my father how to read.

At that time, he could only read at the six-grade level.

My mother helped my father become an outstanding man.

I always wondered how my father was able to sell himself to my mother and what was the motive. To me they always seemed as different as the North and South Pole.

So, one day I got up the courage to ask my mom, and she said, "I recognized he had good blood in his veins, and he had possibilities that I believed I could bring out in him."

My mother did bring them out in my father. My father became an outstanding diesel mechanic.

Mrs. Henry Ford and Mrs. Thomas A. Edison are two more outstanding examples Mr. Hill used to show what a woman can do to make her husband successful. Had it not been for Mrs. Ford's understanding of the mastermind principle, although Mr. Hill said she did not call it by that name, I doubt Mr. Ford would have been known, and I doubt the Ford automobile industry would have been ushered in.

It was Mrs. Ford, more than it was Mr. Ford, who kept him alert and kept him filled with confidence in himself.

While all the other people were criticizing him and his contraption, as they called his automobile, saying it was only designed to scare horses, it was Mrs. Ford who sustained him through those trying hours when the going was hard in Mr. Ford's life.

A lot of times a woman will marry a man because she sees that he has possibilities, and she can do something with him. She believes she can help make something of him.

Sometimes it's monetary considerations, and sometimes it's love. Sometimes it's one thing, and sometimes it's another thing.

Anytime anyone engages in any transaction there is a motive behind that transaction. Whatever it is you want anybody to do, pick out the right kind of motive and plant it in the mind of the other person under the proper circumstances. Then you will have become a master salesman.

You will need to adopt a definite plan through which each member of the mastermind alliance will make his or her contribution in working towards achieving the goal of the alliance. Then you must arrange a definite time and definite place for the mutual discussion of the plan. Indefiniteness will bring you defeat.

You need to keep a regular means of contact between all members of your mastermind alliance. Why do you need to do that? Have you ever had a great friendship with someone, then suddenly it grew cold and finally died?

What was the cause? Neglect was the cause.

If you want to have very dear and close friends, the only way to do that is by keeping in contact with them through life, even if it's nothing more than an occasional postal card, e-mail, or Facebook.

The most successful physicians are the ones that mix hope and faith with the medicines they prescribe.

3

APPLIED FAITH

If you have a definite major purpose and know exactly what you want to do in your life, then a mastermind alliance of like-minded people will you achieve your definite major purpose. Then you have enough applied faith to keep you going while you pursue your definite major purpose. Don't you see that's about all you would need to succeed? Then why do you suppose you will need these other fourteen additional principles?

You will need these fourteen additional principles to induce you to make use of these first three. You will need personal initiative, imagination, enthusiasm, and concentration, because this philosophy is something like a recipe for baking a cake.

When you go to bake a cake, you don't just put one ingredient into the cake, you put in a pinch of this and a pinch of that and a dash of the other, and you put it into the oven and bake the ingredients.

If you took out any one of these other fourteen principles, you wouldn't have the same kind of a cake. These remaining fourteen principles are supporting principles of the first three.

Faith is a state of mind that has been properly called the mainspring of the soul through which one's aims, desires, plans, and purposes may be translated into their physical or financial equivalent.

Applied faith is something vastly different from just mere belief in things. The word applied means what?

The word "applied" is the action part of applied faith, and without action, faith is nothing more than day-dreaming.

There are many people in the world that believe in things, but none of them do anything about it. These people are only engaging in daydreaming.

The Fundamentals of Applied Faith

The fundamentals of applied faith are a definite major purpose supported by personal initiative and applied action.

That means continuous action, not only on your part, but also on the part of those who may be cooperating with you or mastermind allies of yours.

A positive mind free from all negatives such as fear, envy, hatred, jealousy, and greed are essential in your life.

Did you know your mental attitude determines the effectiveness of your applied faith? Did you know that is a fact?

The frame of mind you're in when you go into prayer determines what happens because of that prayer.

You can test this out for yourself and see that this is true.

I'm sure you've had the same experiences I've had of sending out prayers that didn't produce anything but a negative result. You've had that experience at least once in your life, haven't you?

Do you ever suppose there has been anybody who hasn't had that experience at least one time or another in his or her life? When you go to prayer, for it to work you must have absolute positive faith in whatever you're going after or wanting to acquire, and see it in advance in your possession

Before you start to ask for it, the chances are the effect of your prayer will be negative. My mental picture of what happens when you pray properly is you first condition your mind with a definite clear picture of what you desire. Then you transfer over to your subconscious mind a clear picture of what you desire.

The subconscious mind is the intermediary or gatekeeper between you and infinite intelligence. That's the only way you can turn on the power of infinite intelligence. If that isn't correct as far as I'm concerned, it might just as well be correct, because that's the way I get it to work in my book of rules. Recognize the fact every adversity carries with it the seed of an equivalent benefit, and temporary defeat is not failure, until it has been accepted as such.

Do you know where most people fall in their connection with the application of their applied faith? It's when they are defeated, and they accept that defeat as something they can't do anything about reversing.

Instead of immediately beginning to search for the seed of an equivalent benefit that's in every defeat, these people become moody, broody, discouraged, and build up inferiority complexes instead of reversing that order and making another effort.

The subconscious mind only knows what you tell it, what you allow other people to tell it, or what you allow the circumstances of life to tell it.

It doesn't know the difference between a penny and a million dollars. It will accept the things you send over.

If you send over predominating thoughts on poverty, ill health, and failure, that's exactly what you'll get out of your life.

You're going to find out the subconscious mind responds to the mental attitude you're maintaining during the day.

It's necessary for you to affirm repeatedly the goals you are aiming to attain in life, until you educate your subconscious mind to attract automatically to you the things that are related to what you're aiming for in your life.

You're going to find out your mind is like an electromagnet, once you charge it with a clear picture of what you desire. It will attract to you from the highways and byways the things that you will need to carry out that definite major purpose. Then, recognition of the existence of infinite intelligence gives orderliness to the entire universe, and to you the individual that is a minute expression of that intelligence. Your mind has no limitations whatsoever, except those you deliberately set up in your own mind or accept. That's a pretty broad statement isn't it?

The achievements of men such as Mr. Edison, Mr. Carnegie, Mr. Ford, Mr. Hill, and John West, if you please, support the idea the mind has no limitations except those one sets up in his or her own mind or accepts.

I must tell you, if I had ever wavered for just one second from the time I started reading Napoleon Hill's books and listing to his lectures until the time I gave this book to the world in belief I would complete it, I never would have completed it.

Do you have any idea what played the strongest part in what I've achieved in my life? It wasn't my brilliance, and it sure wasn't my outstanding intelligence. I have no more brilliance or intelligence than the average person. There was something responsible for what I have achieved: I believed I could do it, and I never stopped believing. The harder the going was in my life, the more I believed I would accomplish my definite major purpose.

If you can take that kind of positive mental attitude towards yourself when you're overtaken by adversity and defeat, and you have people against you, then you're using applied faith.

Did you know there are testing times for people through life? Nobody can attain a high state in life and stay up there without being tested. Just as nobody can walk into a well-managed business, get a high position, and stay there without being tested, sometimes they might have to work through lower positions step by step until they earn the right to be up at the top.

I don't know how God runs his business entirely, but I can see He allows no one to attain a high state in life without allowing them severe testing. One of the most astounding things I had found in my research was every man and every woman of great achievement in all walks of life throughout the ages. These men and women were great only in proportion to exactly as they were small, had been defeated, has met with opposition, or has had to struggle.

If you knew the major defeats I have met in my life and still lived to keep my head above water and to complete this book, you'd say, "If West did it, I could do it, too." I want you to affirm your definite major purpose in the form of a daily prayer and recognize the existence of infinite intelligence.

You can call that God, or Jehovah, or Buddha, or Mohammed, anything you want to call the first cause. No matter what you call it, we're still talking about the same first cause. There's one first cause that's responsible for this great universe we're living in. It's responsible for you, me, and everything else that's in the universe.

I call it the infinite intelligence because I have friends of all faiths and religions all over the world. Infinite intelligence just happens to be sort of a neutral in-between term that nobody in the world can object to, unless you do not believe in infinite intelligence, and you can put down on paper evidence of a first cause that you can draw upon. You're not going to be able to make the fullest use of applied faith.

My friend Mike asked me one day about my concept of infinite intelligence, if I meant the same thing as God. I said, "Yes, I do mean same thing."

Mike asked me, "Can you prove the existence of your concept of infinite intelligence or God?"

I said, "Everything in the universe is the finest evidence of the existence of God, because of the orderliness of the universe.

Everything orderly, from the electrons and protons of the smallest part of matter to the largest suns that float out in the heavens. Everything in orderliness, no chaos and no running together of the planets. There's more evidence of a first cause than in anything I know about in the world.

If you don't believe it, don't accept it, don't see it, don't feel it, then you won't know you're a minute part of that infinite intelligence expressing that presence through your brain. Once you recognize that, then you will recognize the truth of what I just said. Your only limitations are those you set up in your own mind, permit somebody else to set up, or the circumstances of life to establish.

Did you know your adversities are your greatest blessings?

Do you have any idea the greatest blessing that ever came into my life? It was my divorce and my son being taken away from me while I was doing my research for this book.

I'll tell you why that's my greatest blessing. I found my other self, and it gave me the strength, wisdom, and ability to complete this book. I've had many other adversities in my life. Without the major adversities I have gone through in my life, I would never have been able to prove the soundness of this philosophy, and that there is a seed of an equivalent benefit in every defeat.

Can you see any benefit or imagine any worst adversity coming to a man just getting married and being involved in a car accident, then waking up several days later in a hospital in the emergency room with tubes stuffed down his throat on a machine keeping him alive? I'm always thankful that happened because of my contact with infinite intelligence. I was kept alive to do some great work for our country. I got my greatest demonstration of the power of faith. I never accepted I was going to have medical problems the rest of my life. I'm living a perfectly healthy and normal life which proves any kind of an adversity can be transmuted into a benefit.

You just reading this won't mean a thing to you in the world, unless you begin to look at your own experiences and take inventory of what happens to you in the future.

There may be some things happening to you in the future that are unpleasant. Maybe some to me, too. I can tell you what I'm going to do when anything unpleasant happens to me.

I'm going to immediately transmute the unpleasant experience into something pleasant. Then self-respect expressed through harmony with one's own conscience is certainly an important factor in applied faith.

Isn't that a great thing God put in everyone a judge advocate that tells them right from wrong? You don't have to ask anybody what's right or wrong, because your own conscience tells you right from wrong, unless, it's converted into a conspirator instead of a co-operator by having it choked off instead of responding to it as so many people do in life. That conscience cannot only be a guide, but it can also be corrupted to where it's a conspirator. A lot of people use it just for that definite purpose. Believe me, they have it choked off. It helps them to cover up their meanness. If that were not true, there wouldn't be so many brutes all over the world concocting plans for starting bigger and more devastating wars.

Here is what you must do to achieve your goals in life

You will need to decide on what your desires are and determine what you will have to give in return for what your desires are in your life. What kind of house do you want to live in? What kind of car do you want to drive to school or work? What kind of wardrobe do you want to wear? What kind of an education do you want to have or how many children to have if you want them? What kind of a present are you going to buy your wife on her birthday?

(You'd better buy her one often if you want to keep on good terms with her and stay married.) What kind of cake do you want to bake your husband on his birthday? (You better bake a good one.)

Did you know it's not the big things in a relationship between a man and his wife that count? It's the little things in a relationship that count most, the little things a wife cooks up for her husband. I don't mean only in the food, but it's the little parties, the little visits, and the little trips that women "cook up" for a man. They don't amount to so much in one way, and yet in another way, they're very sentimental. That keeps the relationship alive that you had before you asked her to marry you.

How do you keep your relationship strong and your prayers answered? You get into the habit of prayer when you don't need anything. What do you pray for then? You give gratitude for what you already have in your life.

Wouldn't it be interesting if I gave you a fun assignment today to write down everything you have in this world to be thankful for? I'm giving you that assignment. It's going to be one of the biggest shocks of your life. You can certainly start with the fact you are associated here in a country where we have freedom of speech, freedom of action, freedom of thought, and freedom of opportunity.

I want you to keep your mind open for guidance from within.

What do I mean by that, do you suppose? A hunch, and you get these hunches. Don't be too disrespectful of these hunches that come to you. Treat them with civility and examine them. You will find out these unusual hunches are bringing you messages to get you over the hump of whatever you're doing.

When you're inspired by some hunch to move on some plan created by your imagination, which leads in the direction you desire. Accept the plan, and act upon the plan at once. Remember, there can be no such state of mind as applied faith without appropriate action, because faith without deeds is dead.

When you're overtaken by defeat as you may be overtaken by defeat many times in your life, remember a man's faith is tested many times and your defeat may be only one of your testing times. Isn't that an outstanding and encouraging thing to recognize? When you're meeting with defeat or overtaken by defeat, you're only being tested to see if you're a man or

John West

a worm. And believe me, we all go through that testing time.

The ones who survive these tests with an abiding faith are the ones that become truly great in life. There's no doubt in the world it was a part of God's plan to see that anybody that amounts to anything above mediocrity must undergo paying the price of test after test of their faith. There's no doubt about that, because I see evidence everywhere that this is true. Not taking full control of your mind will destroy the power of your faith and will result in a negative climax of any affirmation you express.

Your mind is everything.

The only thing you have full control over in this world is your mind. That strictly connotes the fact God intended your mind to be the most important asset you have in your life. It is the most important asset you have, because with the use of that mind you can project it into any objective or toward the attainment of any end you choose.

Your education, your background, your nationality, and your creed have nothing to do with your ability to achieve things. It's taking control of your mind and start using that great mind that determines how, what, and when one achieves things.

To me, the most profound thing in all the knowledge of mankind is the fact the humblest person can take control of their mind. He or she can project that mind into high places or can project that mind into the gutter. He or she can make themselves a success or can make themselves a failure. Just taking control of one's mind and start using that great mind changes from failure into success almost instantly. A burning desire is the stuff faith is created out of, and there are many desires in the world.

Most people in their whole life never experience a burning desire for anything. We start out with hopes, not very definite hopes, but faint hopes for things, then wishes.

Everybody wishes for a lot of money without having to work for money. My friends reading this book know you must earn things before you can have money. Most people wish for a new car when they're driving a used one.

If you want a new car, and you make up your mind to have one, you will have to see if the men or the women working under you or the job you're holding will entitle you to drive a nice new car. If you don't want a nice new car, then chances are you'll drive a used one or something less the rest of your life. You must want things with a burning desire and then you must do something about that burning desire. What is it?

You must start right where you stand in showing that you do have faith in your ability with action. Here is one example of a woman of great achievement: Ms. Helen Keller, who believed she would learn to talk despite the fact she had lost the use of her speech, her sight, and her hearing in her early life.

Ms. Helen Keller became one of the best-educated women in the world. Ms. Keller was in contact with more public affairs, civic affairs, and conditions all over the world than nine out of ten women who had all their senses. If you spoke to her, she would put her fingertips up to your lips, so she could tell what you were saying entirely by vibration.

Can you imagine a woman with a handicap of that kind going all the way through life rendering useful service by making speeches she had learned after a fashion to talk? Ms. Helen Keller was doing great work where most women would have settled for a tin cup and a bunch of lead pencils on the street corner with any one of those afflictions.

While Mr. Hill was on the staff of Franklin D. Roosevelt, he passed every day on his way to the White House a man on a street corner trying to eke out a living by begging.

Mr. Hill got acquainted with that man and found that this man was better educated and had the same affliction as Franklin D. Roosevelt. Here was a better-educated man settling for a tin cup and a bunch of lead pencils on the street corner, and another man with the most responsible position in the whole world running a great nation who had also lost the use of his legs. But he didn't lose confidence in himself or in his brain.

The afflictions that come along in our life turn out to be a great blessing. Very often they teach us that we can get along without an eye or without both eyes or without legs or without hands. We can get along without a lot of things if we have the right positive mental attitude toward what's left of us.

How do you suppose you keep your mind off the things you don't desire? I want you to look up that word "transmute" in the dictionary and see what it means. You may know in a general way but look it up because it will be more impressive in your subconscious mind. The way you keep your mind from the things you don't desire is to transmute your thoughts over to the things you do desire. You should start giving thanks for already possessing them, and that won't sound silly to you, because you know what you're doing.

You're reeducating yourself and keeping your mind focused on things you desire. If you ever feel blue, discouraged, or lacking in courage, I will give you a good remedy to cure your problem: You sit down with a tablet and start numbering number one the thing you want most in your life. Then assign number two to the thing you want next most in your life. Next, number three, the thing you want most after that and so on.

Also, when it comes to the kind of a house you want to live in, describe what kind of lot you want it on. Describe if you want it on a lot of acreage or on top of a hill. Describe if you want it down below the road or above the road. Describe how many rooms you want in that house, and how you want each room furnished. You will have a great time furnishing those rooms. That becomes better than window-shopping because you can go the limit in your own mind.

Do some mental window-shopping, and believe me, you'll get your mind off that moodiness and onto something that's constructive.

You will be educating your subconscious mind to keep on the right side of the street and away from the other side of the railroad tracks.

I'm going to give you a fun assignment, and you will get great joy out of physically writing things down when anything bothers you or upsets you in any way. I don't know why when a person finally decides to get what they desire.

The powers of the universe seem to come to their aid. I don't know why that's true, but it is, and that's enough for me. There are many things in my life I can see and many advantages I can use that I don't understand. I don't need to understand them. I know which row of buttons to press on my desk to get the results that I want. I don't need to know what happens between the pressing of that button and the result that does happen. I know if you will follow the instructions in this philosophy, you can get the things out of life you desire, and you can make life pay off point by point on your own terms instead of accepting mere circumstances.

How do I know any individual can make life pay off on their own terms instead of accepting the circumstances?

I can tell you as sincerely as I'm writing the pages of this book. There isn't a blessed thing I want or can't get easily in my life. That's such an astounding statement, because it's so broadly in contrast to what I might have several years back before I had finally learned the "secret formula" of getting everything I want in my life.

There is no such thing as a blanket faith. You must have a definite objective, purpose, and goal before you can have applied faith to have faith in anything. Faith is a positive mental attitude wherein your mind is cleared of all fears and doubts and directed toward the attainment of a definite major purpose through the inspiration of infinite intelligence.

Faith will do nothing for you if you expect everything to be done outside of yourself, because faith is only guidance. If you're definite major purpose is to achieve material things or money, start picturing or seeing yourself already in possession of the money or thing you desire when you call it into your consciousness. This is of vital importance because here again comes into play your power of applied faith. If your applied faith isn't great enough to see the thing you desire already in your possession before you start asking for what you desire, then you're not making the fullest use of applied faith.

You've had this experience where you wanted something very badly, and to get to that something meant extra money you couldn't get your hands on. You weren't earning it, so what do you do in a case of that kind? You begin to connive and scheme some way to earn some money, don't you?

I remember when I was a small boy I wanted a fancy baseball glove that cost a hundred dollars. That was a lot of money that my parents couldn't afford to pay at that time.

I took the push lawn mower out of the shed and went down the street mowing enough lawns to earn my hundred dollars. My brother and sister thought I was crazy for doing that just for a baseball glove. I say, crazy my eye; they should have realized what kind of kid their parents produced.

I want you to keep yourself inspired by the nine basic motives when you go after anything worthwhile. I want you to learn to write down a list of all the advantages of your definite major purpose, and call these into your mind many times daily, thereby making your mind success conscious. You do know that to be healthy, you must be health conscious. If you're not thinking in terms of health and not expecting yourself to be healthy, then chances are you won't be healthy.

It's that same thing with success because if you accept any kind of inferiority complex and do not develop a successful expectation of yourself, then chances are you're not going to be a success. Learn to associate with close people who are in sympathy with you and your definite major purpose. Lead these people to encourage you in every which way possible in your life. Never let one single day pass without making at least one definite move toward the attainment of your definite major purpose. Your positive mental attitude speaks louder than your words, and your positive mental attitude is the sum of your thoughts at a given time. A positive mental attitude has its roots in the spiritual wells of one's soul.

Start looking around, and you will see something that suggests a positive mental attitude. You will notice if you go into the office of a successful man or woman or into the home of a successful man or woman, it's surrounded with pictures of men and women they consider great. They do that to live in the environment of the great and the positive.

Start in your office, your home, in your business, or maybe in your bedroom where you sleep every night by putting something up that will give you a positive thought just before you go to bed each night. You will be surprised at how much good that will do for you and keep your mind more positive.

It is a striking coincidence that American ends with "I can."

4

GOING THE EXTRA MILE

I don't know of any one quality or any one trait that can get an individual an opportunity quicker than to go out of his or her way to do somebody a favor and something useful for somebody. It is one thing you can do that you don't ask anybody for the privilege of doing. If you want to be free and are going to be free, self-determining, and financially independent in old age, you might as well accept the fact that you can never be that, except by a stroke of good luck, or a rich aunt or uncle dies.

However, you can form the habit of going the extra mile and make yourself as near to indispensable as you possibly can in the world. I don't know how anybody can make him or herself indispensable except by going the extra mile.

That means rendering some sort of service one is not expecting and rendering that service in the right sort of positive mental attitude. That mental attitude is very important, because if you gripe about going the extra mile, the chances are it won't bring you many profitable returns.

John West

Where do you suppose I get my authority do you suppose that causes me to emphasize the principle of going the extra mile?

I get it by looking around and watching the way that nature does things. Any time you can follow the habits of nature, you cannot go wrong. Any time you fail to recognize the way nature does things and do not go along, you will run into trouble sooner or later in your life. There is an overall plan in which this universe operates, and there's just one plan. There's just one set of natural laws, and it's up to every individual to discover what those natural laws are and adjust themselves favorably to them. If there's one thing that stands out above all others in nature, it's the fact nature requests and demands that every living thing go the extra mile to eat, live, and survive.

Man could not survive one season if it weren't for the law of going the extra mile. You can't render a million dollars' worth of service a day and expect to get a bank check in the morning. If you start out to render a million dollars' worth of service, you will have to render it a little bit at a time. You will have to get yourself recognized and received, and chances are you will not be compensated for going the extra mile for quite a little while. The chances are you will have to go the extra mile for quite a while before any one will ever take notice of the service you are rendering.

You will need to always be careful you don't go the extra mile too long without the right person taking notice of the service that you are rendering. If the right person doesn't take notice of the service you are rendering, start looking around until you do find the right person who will take notice of the service you are rendering. That's the equivalent of saying if your present employer doesn't recognize the service you are rendering, fire the employer and let his competitor know what kind of service you are rendering. That won't hurt your chances a bit, and you can have a little fun competition as you go along. Nobody ever accepts a rule or does anything without a motive.

I will give you a great variety of reasons why you should go the extra mile, so you can benefit by the law of increasing returns. What does the law of increasing returns mean? The law of increasing returns means when you go out of your way to render more service and better service than you're paid to render, it's impossible for you not to get back more. That's the way the law of nature works, because whatever you give out comes back to you greatly multiplied in kind. The coming-back process doesn't always come back very quickly, and sometimes it's longer than you expected.

If you send out some negative influence, it's going to come back to you sooner or later in your life.

It won't overlook you because the law of increasing returns is eternal, automatic, and working all the time. It's just as inexorable as the law of gravity, and there's nobody in the world that can circumvent the law of increasing returns or have it suspended for any length of time. It's impossible for you to not get back more than you really did, because eventually the law of increasing return will take care of the service you're rendering.

If you're working for a salary, it will take care of it in a larger salary, and in greater responsibilities and greater opportunities for you to go into business for yourself. The law of increasing returns comes back in 1,001 different ways. The coming-back process does not always come back from the source to which you rendered the service.

Don't be afraid to render service to a greedy buyer or greedy employer.

If you render the service in good faith and in good spirit and keep on doing it as a matter of habit, it's just as impossible for you not to be compensated as it is to be compensated at the same time. Just remember, when you start applying the principle of going the extra mile, you don't have to be careful to whom you render the service.

What you should really do is apply this principle with every person you meet no matter who it is—strangers, acquaintances, business associates, and relatives alike. The only way you can increase the space you occupy in the world—and I mean the physical space, the mental space, and spiritual space—will be determined by the quality and the quantity of the service you render and the mental attitude in which you render the service.

These are the determining factors as to how far you will go in life:

How much you will get out of life.

How much you will enjoy life.

How much peace of mind you will have in life.

Then that brings one to the favorable attention of those who can and often do provide opportunities for self-promotion. You go into any organization, and if you're alert minded, you will find out very quickly the people who are going the extra mile. If you watch the procedure and records of the people who are going the extra mile, you will find out when the promotions come around, they're the ones who get the promotion. They don't have to ask for the promotion because employers are just naturally looking around for people who will go the extra mile. Then it also tends to permit one to become indispensable in many different forms of human relationships, and therefore enables one to demand more than the average compensation.

I will tell you one thing it does for you: it does something for your soul inside of you that makes you feel better. If there weren't another reason in the world why you should go the extra mile, then I would say that would be adequate.

There many things in life that cause us to have negative feelings and cause us to have unpleasant experiences and unpleasant feelings. This is one thing that you can do for yourself that will always give you a pleasant feeling. I'm sure you never did anything kind for someone that you didn't get a great deal of joy out of going the extra mile for the other person. Most probably or maybe the other person didn't appreciate you going the extra mile, but that's unimportant because it's just like love.

To have loved alone is a great privilege, and it makes no difference whatsoever if the other person returns your love.

You still had the benefit by the emotion of love itself, and it's the same thing with the principle of going the extra mile. It will do something for you, and it will give you greater courage, enabling you to overcome these inhibitions, and those inferiority complexes that you have been storing up through the years just by your stepping out and making yourself useful to somebody.

Don't become too surprised when you do something courteous or useful, and they look at you in a quizzical way. Some people will be a little bit surprised when you go out of your way to be useful to them. That will lead you to mental growth and physical perfection in various forms of different services, thereby developing greater ability and skill in one's chosen vocation. Or like filling your job or completing a task or making up your notebook or delivering a lecture, or writing a book, or whatever it is you're going to do that you're going to keep repeating.

You should make up your mind that every time you

do it, you're going to exceed all previous efforts on your part and be a constant challenge to yourself.

I've never done anything in my life I didn't intend to do better than I previously started out to do. I don't always do it, but that's my intention. It makes no difference what kind of job or what kind of task I'm doing or if I'm helping another person. I want to be useful; I want to grow; and I want to develop. Out of effort, out of struggle, and out of use of your faculties comes growth. That enables you to profit by the law of contrast. Had you ever thought about that? I tell you right now you won't have to advertise that one, because that will advertise itself. Most people around you will not be going the extra mile, and that's all the better for your benefit. If everybody in the world went the extra mile, what a grand world it would be to live in.

You couldn't cash in on this principle as definitely as you can cash in on it now because you'd have a tremendous amount of competition. Don't worry; you're not going to have any competition, and you will practically be in a class all by yourself. There may be some cases perhaps to where the people with whom you're working or the people you're associated with will be shown up for not going the first mile, let alone the second mile, and they won't like what you're doing. So, of course, you're going to cry about that and quit and go back to your old habits just because the other person doesn't like what you're doing or are you? Of course, you're not.

Listen, my friend, it's your individual responsibility in the world to succeed. That's your sole responsibility, and you can't afford to let anyone's ideas, idiosyncrasies, or notions get in the way of your success. You should be fair and just with other people, but beyond that, you're under no obligation to let anyone's opinions or ideas stop you from going out in the world and becoming successful.

I'd like to see the person that could stop me from being successful, and I'd love to look at them and see what they look like.

I want you to feel that same way and to make up your mind you're going to put these laws into operation; you're not going to let anybody stop you from using them. That will lead you to the development of a positive, pleasing mental attitude, which is among the most important traits of a pleasing personality, as you will see when you get to chapter five. Isn't it a great thing to know what you can do to change the chemistry of your brain so you're more positive than you are negative? Isn't it a great thing to know you can do that so easily?

By starting in the frame of mind where you want to do something useful for the other person, without rendering service with one hand and picking their pocket with the other hand, while you're rendering useful service. Doing it just because of the goodness you get out of rendering useful service by knowing that eventually when you render more service and better service, then sooner or later, you'll be paid for more than you do and paid willingly. That's the law of compensation, and the law of compensation is an eternal law because it never forgets. It has a perfectly marvelous bookkeeping system, and you may be sure when you're giving out the right kind of service and the right kind of positive mental attitude. You're piling up credits for yourself somewhere that will come back to you greatly multiplied.

Then, it also develops a keen alert imagination, because it's a habit that keeps one continuously seeking new and more efficient ways of rendering useful service. It develops your imagination, and you begin to look around and see how many other ways and means there are in helping other people to find him or herself.

Incidentally, one of the most outstanding things I discovered in my research is if you have a problem or an unpleasant situation and you don't know how to solve the problem. If you have done everything you know anything about, and you've tried every source you know anything about, and you're still at a stalemate, there is always one thing you can do. If you'll do that one thing, the chances are you will solve your problem. Find somebody who has an equal or greater problem and start where you stand to help that other person.

Lo and behold, it unlocks some cells of the brain and permits infinite intelligence to come into your brain and give you the solution to the answer of your problem.

I don't know what it does to you, and I don't know why it works. There are a lot of things I don't know, and there are a lot of things you don't know about. That's one thing I don't know anything about, but I do something about it, and I follow the law. If I need my own mind to be opened to receive opportunities, the best way in the world to open my mind and receive opportunities is to start looking around and see how many other people I can help solve their problems. That gets you into the habit of looking around for something useful to do and going out and doing something useful without somebody telling you to go out and do something useful.

You know old man procrastination is a sour old bird. He causes a lot of problems and a lot of trouble in the world by causing people to put off things until the day after tomorrow, which they should have done the day before yesterday. We're all guilty of it.

I'm now freer of procrastination than I was a few years back, I can tell you that for sure. Why can I say I'm freer of procrastination, and why can I find a lot of things to do now? I get a lot of joy out of doing them, and anytime you're going the extra mile, you're going to get great joy out of what you're doing. Then it serves to build the confidence in others of one's integrity and general ability.

It aids one in mastering the destructive habit of procrastination. It develops a definite major purpose without which one cannot hope for success.

Going the extra mile gives you an objective, so you don't always go around in circles like a goldfish in a bowl, always coming back to where you started without anything.

A definite major purpose comes out of the business of going the extra mile.

I'll tell you another thing a definite major purpose does is it enables you to make your work a joy instead of a burden in life, and you get to where you love your work. I think that if you're not engaged in a labor of love you're just wasting a lot of your time. I think one of the greatest joys in the world is being permitted to engage in the one thing one would rather do than all other things. Surely when you're going the extra mile, you're doing exactly that, because you don't have to go the extra mile. Nobody expects you to go the extra mile and nobody asked you to go the extra mile.

Certainly, no employer would ask his or her employee to go the extra mile. Oh, he or she might ask to help occasionally, but as a regular thing, they wouldn't ask anybody to go the extra mile. It's something you do on your own personal initiative, and it gives you dignity even if you're doing nothing but digging a ditch or driving a bus or a truck or working in a department store.

You're going the extra mile just because you're helping somebody, and you have a certain amount of dignity attached to the labor. That takes all the fatigue and all the unpleasantness out of the labor you're doing. What is the most important application you ever made in your entire life of going the extra mile out of which you got the greatest amount of joy?

How about before getting married?

Believe me, I've spent a lot of time burning midnight oil. I didn't consider it hard work. I not only used my personal initiative, but I also got a lot of joy out of burning the midnight oil. It's amazing how long you can go when you're courting the girl of your choice or being courted by the man of your choice, and how much sleep you can lose and still not be seriously hurt by losing the sleep.

Wouldn't it be a wonderful thing if you could put the same attitude into your relationship with people in your business that you put into courtship? We're all going to start back sparking again and we're going to start at home with our own mates. That will save you a lot of friction and a lot of arguments in your relationship, and it cuts down your expenses. I'm very serious when I say it's one of the finest places in the world to start going the extra mile.

When you start going the extra mile with somebody you hadn't been going the extra mile with, sit down and have a little sales talk with him or her. Tell them you want an agreement for both parties to change their mental attitude, and from here on out all of us are going to start going the extra mile.

We're all going to each on a different basis where

we'll all get great joy out of going the extra mile and get more peace of mind and more happiness in living. Wouldn't it be a wonderful thing to have that kind of speech with your mate? The mate might not be too impressed by your speech, but you sure will be impressed by your speech.

Then that person in business you haven't been getting along so well with, in the past, and you went into work with a smile on your face in the morning. You walk up to him or her and shook their hand and said, "Now, listen here, my friend, from here on out lets you and me enjoy working together." Don't be afraid to humiliate yourself if it's going to build up some better relations with the other people you associate with every day. Do you know going the extra mile is the only way you have the right to ask for a promotion or for more pay or get a better job?

You don't have a leg to stand on in going into the purchaser of your services and asking for more money or for a promotion to a better job unless for some time you have been previously going the extra mile. Obviously, [f you're doing no more than you're paid for, then you're being paid for all you're entitled to, aren't you? So, you must first start going the extra mile to put the other person under obligation to you before you can ask any favors of them

I'll tell you one thing, if you have enough people whom you have put under obligation to you by going the extra mile, when you need some favor, you can always turn one direction or the other direction and receive a favor.

I want you to have that kind of extra credit with other people.

Soundness of going the extra mile

We get our cue to the soundness of the principle of going the extra mile by observing Mother Nature and how she goes the extra mile. Nature goes the extra mile by producing enough of everything for her needs as well as a surplus for emergencies and waste, such as the blooms on the trees, and the fishes in the seas and in the rivers. She doesn't just produce enough fish to perpetuate the species; she produces enough to feed the snakes and the alligators and everything else that dies of natural causes.

Nature is most bountiful in her business of going the extra mile, and in return she is very demanding in seeing every living creature go the extra mile. Bees are provided with honey as compensation for their services in fertilizing the flowers in which the honey is attractively stored. They must perform the service to get the honey, and it must be performed in advance.

You've heard it said, the birds of the air and the beasts of the jungle neither weave nor spin but they always live and eat. If you will observe wildlife, they don't eat without performing some sort of service or without doing service before they can eat safely. Take a flock of common cornfield crows. They must organize and have sentinels put down for their protection. They travel in flocks, have codes to warn one another, and must do a lot of educating before they can eat safely.

Nature requires man to go the extra mile and must go out and plant the seed in the ground, if he's going to have food to eat. All food comes from the ground. A man's got to plant the seed in the ground, because he can't live entirely on what nature plants. At least, not in civilized life, you can't, or maybe over on the islands or some other place that's not civilized. I suppose they still depend on eating raw coconuts.

In civilized life, we must plant our food in the ground. We must clear the ground and harrow it. We must put a fence up to protect it against predatory animals and so forth.

All that costs labor, time, and money, and it must be done in advance, or a man's not going to eat or have anything to sell at the market.

I wouldn't have any trouble selling the idea to a farmer. Nature makes him go the extra mile. The farmer knows every minute of his life, if he doesn't go the extra mile he doesn't eat, and he doesn't have anything to sell at the market.

A new employee, for instance, going into a new job can't come right in and start going the extra mile, then immediately demand top wages or the best job in the place.

You must establish a record and a reputation and get yourself recognized and received in the business of going the extra mile to get compensation back for going the extra mile. As a matter of fact, if you go the extra mile in the right sort of positive mental attitude, chances are a thousand to one you will never have to ask for compensation according to the service you render.

That will be tendered to you automatically in the way of a promotion or increased salary.

Throughout the whole universe, everything has been so arranged through the law of compensation so adequately described by Emerson. Nature's budget is balanced, so to speak. Everything has its opposite equivalent in something else. Like positive and negative, in every unit of energy, day and night, hot and cold, success and failure, sweet and sour, happiness and misery, man and woman.

Everything you do, everything you think, and every thought you release causes a reaction. When you release a thought, you're not through with the thought, because every thought you express silently becomes a definite part of the pattern of your subconscious mind. If you store in your subconscious mind enough negative thoughts, you will be predominantly negative all the time. If you follow the habit of releasing only the positive thoughts, your subconscious pattern will be predominantly positive, and you will attract to you all the things you desire most.

The business of going the extra mile is one of the finest ways I know of educating your subconscious mind to attract to you all the things you desire and to repel all the things you don't desire. You can put it down as an established fact that if you neglect to develop and apply the principle of going the extra mile, you will never become personally successful and will never become financially independent.

The reason I happen to know what sound is, because I've had an experience you haven't had yet, but you will have in time. I've had the great privilege of finding out what has happened to people who have applied the principle of going the extra mile. I know beyond any question of a doubt nobody ever rises above ordinary stations in life or mediocrity without the habit of going the extra mile.

If I ever did discover just one case in my research where somebody has gone to the top without going the extra mile, then I would say there are exceptions. I'm able to say there are no exceptions because I have never found that one case.

I can tell you from my own experiences, and I've been there every minute of my life. I have never had any major benefit of any kind in the world that I didn't get it as the result of going the extra mile. That's the thing I want you to do—to become self-determining so you can do these things without the help of anybody. That's the time when the payoff will come in your life when you can go out in the world and can do anything you want to do whether anybody wants to help you, or they don't help you, and you can do it on your own.

I want to tell you the most glorious feeling I know anything about is whatever I want to do I can do, and I don't have to ask anybody. If I did have to ask someone, I would, because I'm on good terms with everybody.

Then, here is a little item not to be sniffed at too lightly.

It's the peace of mind I got out of all this work going the extra mile.

Do you have any idea how many people there are in the world at any one time willing to do anything years in succession without being sure they are going to get something back? Do you have any idea how many people there are in the world willing to do anything three days in succession without being sure they are going to get something back?

You'd be surprised if you found out how few people there are in the world. Most people overlook one of the grandest opportunities a human being could possibly have, especially here in a country where we can create our own destiny.

We can express ourselves in any way we want to express ourselves. Speech is free, physical activities are free, and public libraries are free. It's a wonderful opportunity to go the extra mile in any direction you want to travel. Yet, most people are not going the extra mile, and it almost seems today everybody has troubles, or thinks he or she has troubles.

Do you know how I spend all my time instead of finding out what's wrong with the rest of the world? I try to find out what I can do to correct this guy here, because I must eat with him. I must sleep him. I must shave his face in the morning. I must give him a bath. I have so many things I have to do for him. I try to use my spare time helping my friends by writing this book. It sure does pay off a lot better than if I spent all my time reading all the murder stories across the newspapers, all the divorce scandals, violence and crime, and all other junk embezzled across the newspapers every day. I'm still talking about this country guy from Kansas who didn't have sense enough not to go the extra mile for the richest man in the world.

If I had my life to live over again, I would live my life exactly the way I have lived it. I would make all the mistakes I have made and would have made them at the time in my life when I did make them. The period where I come into peace of mind and understanding is in the afternoon of life.

When a man or woman is younger, they can work more hours and take a lot more. As you get older, and when you pass the noon hour and go into the afternoon, your energies are not as great as they were before. Your physical energies, and maybe your mental capacity, is not as great. You can't take as much trouble as you could in the days of your youth You really haven't got many years left to correct the mistakes you have made.

To have the tranquility and the peace of mind I have today in the afternoon of life is one of the greatest joys that have come out of this philosophy. If you ask me what has been my greatest compensation, I would say that's it because there are still many people in the world searching for peace of mind, and they're looking for it in the wrong places.

Peace of mind is something you will have to earn for yourself, because that's how anybody can get it.

You'd really surprised at where you really must start looking for it. It's not out where the average person is looking for it—in the joys of what fame, fortune, or money can buy. It's in the humility of one's own heart. I get peace of mind mostly in the third inner wall I will describe to you when you get to the chapter on self-discipline. That wall is as high as eternity that I go into for meditation many times each day. I can cut out every earthly influence and commune with the higher forces of the universe. You can do that, too, because when you get through reading this book. You will be able to do anything just as well or better than I can do things.

I'm hoping everyone reading this book will excel me in every way possible. Maybe you will take over where I left off in writing books and write a better book than this one.

Why not? I haven't said the last word. I'm just a student.

I think an intelligent student. I'm just a student on the right path, and the only state of perfection I have found is peace of mind and how to get peace of mind. You should engage in at least one act of going the extra mile each day.

You can choose your own circumstance, if it's nothing more than telephoning an acquaintance and wishing them good fortune.

You will be surprised at what happens when you begin to call up your friends you have been neglecting for some time and say, "Hello, you were on my mind. I was just thinking about you, and I just wanted to call you up to see how you're doing."

It doesn't have to be a close friend, because it can be somebody that you know in your life. You might want to relieve some friend from duty for half an hour or so, or have some neighbor send their children over while you let them attend the movies.

You may want to do a little babysitting for one of your neighbors next door. You're going to be home, so maybe you've got some children of your own and you know some neighbor you could relieve, so they could go out and attend a movie.

Oh, I know the children are noisy, and they will probably fight with your children. It'd be a nice thing if you didn't have any children to say, "Could I come over to your house and babysit for you awhile, so you and your husband can go on a little courtship and go out to the movies?"

You will have to know your neighbor well to do that, but certainly you have some neighbor you could approach on that basis, and they wouldn't think you're crazy. Did you know it's not so much as what you do for the other person, but it's what you do for yourself by going the extra mile in little ways?

Did you know that both the successes and the failures in life are made up of such small things? So very little, in fact oftentimes, they're overlooked, because the real things that make up success are such small seemingly insignificant things.

"Kindness is more powerful than compulsion."

5

A PLEASING PERSONALITY

I want to introduce you to the most intelligent and most wonderful person in the world, the person reading this book.

When you start to break down that person point by point in accordance with these twenty-five factors that go into making a pleasing personality, you will find out exactly where and why you're an intelligent and wonderful person. You can grade yourself on these and give yourself the rating you think you are entitled.

You can rate yourself on a scale of 0 to 100, with 100 as the most pleasing. When you get through, add up the total and divide it by the twenty-five traits. This will give you your average rating on the pleasing personality. If you rate all the way through a general rating of 50 percent, you're doing very well.

1. Positive mental attitude

The first trait of a pleasing personality is always a positive mental attitude.

If you don't have a positive mental attitude, at least

when you're in the presence of other people, you're not going to be considered to have a pleasing personality.

You can rate yourself anywhere from zero to a hundred.

If you can rate 100 percent, that's high.

2. Flexibility

This means the ability to unbend and adjust to all the varying circumstances of life.

Do you know how successful people get ahead quickly and become more popular?

They can be all things to all people and do it by adjusting themselves to the mental attitude of other people, and not getting mad at the same time the other person gets mad.

If you want to get mad, do it when you're alone and on your own, or when the other person is in a good humor. That will give you a much better chance of not getting hurt.

There are many things in life you will have to adjust to and be flexible on if you're going to get peace of mind and good health.

3. A pleasing tone of voice

If you're going to teach, lecture, do any public speaking, or just ordinary converse, you can always learn to give a pleasant tone to your voice. If you can't do that or you don't know how to do it, you can do it with a little bit of practice, oftentimes, by simply lowering your voice and not talking too loudly. You can make your voice something pleasing to the other person's ear. I don't think anybody can teach another person how to make his or her tone of voice pleasing. I think it's something you must do by experimenting, but first you must feel pleasing.

How can you use a pleasant tone of voice when you feel angry, or you don't like the person you're talking to?

You can fake it, but it's not too effective unless you really feel inside of you the way you are expressing yourself.

There are techniques you can acquire to make yourself pleasing. I don't know of anything else that will pay off better than to be pleasing in the eyes of other people. It's one of those things you can't get along without it.

4. Tolerance

This means an open mind on all subjects toward all people always. You're always willing to hear the last word or hear additional words someone is saying.

There are some people so close-minded, you couldn't get in a new idea even if you were God. To have a pleasant mental attitude, you've got to have an open mind.

Why should you keep your mind open? Because the very minute people find out you have any prejudices that involve them in their understanding of religion, politics, economics, or anything else that affects them, they're going to dislike you and always get on the other side of the street when they see you coming.

Do you know why I can have followers of all religions read my book, and I get along so well with all of them? To me they are all one brand, my fellow brothers and sisters. I never think of anybody in terms of what he or she believes politically, religiously, or economically. I think of them in terms of what they are trying to do to help themselves or to help other people achieve things.

If you don't keep your mind open, you're not going to learn as much. That means you cease to grow. When you close your mind up against any person or subject and say you don't want additional information on that subject, you cease to grow.

5.   A keen sense of humor

The best medicines I've found to take daily is to have a good laugh several times a day, a good hearty laugh, and if you can't find something to laugh at, looking in a mirror does it for me.

If you have troubles, these will melt away and won't seem near as big as when you're laughing as when you're crying.

I don't know if my sense of humor is keen, but it's alert. I can get fun out of any circumstance. I used to get punishment out of circumstances. I get fun now that I've oiled up and made my sense of humor more alert than it used to be in years past.

6. **Frankness of manner and speech with discriminate control of the tongue always.**

When you start conversing with other people, if you can, say things to benefit the person listening instead of damaging the person listening. That will help your personality.

There are some people who set their mouths to going and go off and leave it open and are almost always in difficulty with somebody. You can't tell everybody what you think of him or her. If you did that, you wouldn't have any friends left in the world, and you need at least one friend.

7. **Pleasing facial expression**

If you studied your facial expressions in the mirror, you can practice making facial expressions better by smiling a little bit.

You will be surprised how much more effective your words can be by smiling when you talk to people instead of frowning or looking serious. I like talking to a person who doesn't have a serious expression on his or her face. That tells me they feel the whole world is on their shoulders, if they limber up and give you a nice million-dollar smile.

Where does a smile take place first, on your lips, your face, or where? In your heart, where you feel it. You don't have to be pretty or handsome.

A smile will decorate you and embellish you no matter who you are and make your facial expression more beautiful.

8. A keen sense of justice toward all people

This means a sense of justice toward all people even when it is to your disadvantage to do so. There's no virtue in being just with the other person when you are the only one benefiting by it.

9. Sincerity of purpose

We all like someone being their self and not being or saying something that doesn't represent his or her inner thoughts. It's not as bad as out-and-out lying, but it's the first cousin to lacking sincerity of purpose.

10. Versatility

Do you have a wide range of knowledge of people and world events outside your personal interest? The man or woman who doesn't know very much except one subject will become a bore to other people the minute they get out of their field.

Have you ever seen or know someone who has their nose too close to the grindstone? How can you make yourself liked by other people? Talk to other people about the things that interest them.

If you do that, then when they get around to talking about things that interest you, these people will have become a much more receptive listener.

11. Tactfulness in speech and manner

When you speak to someone, you don't have to reflect in your mental attitude everything that goes on inside of your mind.

Have you seen these drivers on the road when they skin someone's fender? How tactful they are when they jump out and run around to see how much damage is done?

Maybe only ten cents' worth of paint was knocked off and they do a million dollars' worth of damage cussing the other person out.

Someday I'm going to have the experience of seeing two people collide on the road, and both are going to jump out and apologize to each other, claiming it was both their fault and wanting to split the bill.

You'd be amazed at how much more cooperation you can get from other people if you're just tactful with other people.

Instead of telling people to do things, ask them to do things or request them to do things rather than demand them to do things. It might be very tactful and helpful if you asked them if they would mind doing a certain thing.

The most outstanding employer in the world— Andrew Carnegie—never gave any of his employee's direct instructions.

12. Promptness of decision

Nobody can be very well-liked and have a pleasing personality if they make a habit of putting off deciding on the spot when they have all the facts at hand with which to decide. When you have all the facts at hand and time has arrived for a decision, you should get into the habit of making those decisions. You should never become too big or too little to reverse yourself on a decision.

There is a great advantage in being fair enough with yourself and the other person if you have made the wrong decision.

13. Faith in infinite intelligence

I'm not going to mention much on your faith in infinite intelligence. You should rate 100 percent if you're following your religion faithfully.

Did you know there are a lot of people in the world that just give lip service on that one and don't engage in any outstanding acts?

14. Appropriateness of words free from slang, wisecracks, and profanity.

This age we live in it seems as if we have many people engaged in a lot of wisecracks, slang statements, double talk, and those sorts of things.

I suppose some people may laugh at it, but they're not going to be impressed with a person who engages in wisecracks and smart sayings all the time.

Our English language is not the easiest thing in the world to master, but it is a beautiful language and it does have a wide range of word meanings.

15. Controlled enthusiasm

Your enthusiasm should be handled the way you handle electricity. That electricity washes your dishes in the dishwasher, washes your clothes in the washing machine, runs the toaster, and cooks your food on the stove.

Electricity does a lot of things, and you handle it with care. You can turn it on when you want to turn it on, and you can turn it off when you want to turn it off.

You can be so enthusiastic with the other person that you wear them out and cause them to pull down their sunglasses on you, and try to resist you.

I had a salesman come around my house so enthusiastic I would not let him in my house a second time.

I've heard some speakers and preachers who were like that, and I didn't want to follow them. I had too much trouble resisting them. You know exactly the type of person I'm talking about is the person who just absolutely turns on their enthusiasm battery and leaves it on, and all you can do is run away from it or try to get them to turn it off.

The person who does that is not going to be as popular as the person who can turn on their enthusiasm at the right time and turn it off at the right time and the right place. I think if it's not controlled you might be considered not to have a pleasing personality, but you can cultivate one.

16. Good sportsmanship

You can't win all the time because nobody can win all the time. Lose, and say, "Well, I lost this time, but it's the best thing that has ever happened to me. I'm going to start immediately searching for that seed of an equivalent benefit in every defeat."

Then never take anything too seriously no matter what you're doing.

One of my friends from high school committed suicide. He was depressed, took a gun, and killed himself. I've been depressed before, but I certainly didn't shoot myself.

I said I'd have to learn some more and earn some more.

I told myself if I lose every material thing I own, even the shoes on my feet, I can always walk barefoot or borrow a pair from somebody and start all over again. How are you going to down a man with that kind of a mental attitude?

No matter how many times he's defeated, he'll come right back up again, just like a cork. You can put him down in the water, but he'll bounce up the moment you take your hand off him. If you don't take your hand off him, he'll make you take it off him.

17. Common courtesy

It's great to have common ordinary garden variety of common courtesy toward everybody, and especially towards the people on a lower plane socially, economically, or financially than you are.

I've never liked to go into a restaurant and watching some rich person start ordering the waiters around and abusing them. I have always felt if someone would abuse another person in public with or without a cause had something wrong with his or her machinery. There's something missing in his or her life. As far as I know, I have never intentionally tried to humiliate anybody in public for anything.

You're a human magnet, and you're attracting to you the sum and substance of what goes on in your heart and soul always when you're around other people.

18. Appropriateness of personal adornment

This is always important to someone in public life. I have never ever been very fussy on this one or never used formal clothes except on few occasions. There are times when it's appropriate for you to adjust and have them.

Ordinarily, if you have good taste, the best-dressed person is one dressed so if you were told to describe them later how he or she looked, and you couldn't do it, all you'd say is she looked nice, or he looked nice.

19. Good showmanship

To sell yourself in any walk of life, you can learn to dramatize words and dramatize circumstances. If you took the history of the most outstanding man or women in the world and gave just bare facts as you go along, you'd really fall flat.

You can learn to dramatize things you're talking to people about and to people you're doing business with because showmanship is something you can learn.

20. Going the extra mile

I really don't think I need to mention anything on this one because you have got a whole wonderful chapter on that subject.

21. Temperance

That means not too much and not too little of anything.

I think you can do yourself just as much damage with eating as you can with drinking liquor.

The rule I go by in all things is to never allow anything to take charge of me. There's nothing in life so very good you must overdo it.

22. Patience under all circumstances

You must have a lot of patience in the world, because it's a world of competition. By using patience, you learn to time these things with other people, so you can get action out of them when the time is favorable.

If you don't have any patience and try to force the hand of other people, you will always get a no, a turn-down, or knockdown when you don't want that to happen.

Take the average person, or even most people. You

can make them mad in two seconds. I don't need to get angry because somebody says or does the wrong thing. I could if I wanted to, but it's my choice, and I choose not to get angry.

23. Gracefulness in posture and carriage of the body

Walking around slumped is maybe more comfortable for you, and maybe a lot easier if you have back trouble.

I think it's much more pleasing to eye of others to stand up straight without looking like you must lean on something.

Being careless in your posture marks you as someone who is not very particular about your personal appearance.

24. Humility of the heart based upon a keen sense of modesty

I don't think anything can compare with true humility of the heart. Sometimes I must express disapproval of something somebody is doing. I always say deep down inside of me, "God pity us all, maybe the person I'm criticizing, I've done things ten times as bad of the thing

I'm criticizing them for doing." The more successful I become, the more I observe true humility of the heart.

I fully recognize whatever success I have achieved is due to the friendly love, affection, and cooperation of other people.

25. Personal magnetism

That means sexy motion controlled and directed to beneficial use.

The most outstanding leaders, salesmen, speakers, clergymen, lawyers, lecturers, teachers, the most outstanding in every field of endeavor are the ones who have learned to transmute sexy motion. That means to convert that great creative energy over into doing the thing you want done at the time being.

That word "transmute" is something to consider and to look up in the dictionary to make sure you understand what the word means.

You're going to find when you come down to honestly answering these questions, you found certain weaknesses you didn't know about. You found certain strengths and certain good qualities you had perhaps under-evaluated a little bit.

Let's find out about ourselves and see where we stand, what makes us tick, and why people like or dislike us. Then you can lay your finger right on what's keeping you from being popular if you're not already popular. When you do that, you will have one of the greatest assets you could possibly imagine in the world. The person who receives no pay for their services except that which comes in a pay envelope is underpaid, no matter how much money that envelope may contain.

6

PERSONAL INITIATIVE

This is a great chapter since it's the action-producing portion of the philosophy. It wouldn't make much difference if you understood these principles, and you didn't do anything about them, would it?

The value you're going to get out of this philosophy does not only consist in the information in each one of these chapters that are important. The more important thing is what you will do with all this information. Then start using these ideas, and this philosophy on your own personal initiative. There are certain attributes of initiative and leadership and I would like for you to grade yourself on them. Grading of yourself on these qualities will be the first step toward making these qualities your own.

1. A definite major purpose

If you don't have a definite major overall purpose, then you haven't much personal initiative.

This should be one of the most important steps to take and find out what you want to do with your life. If you're not sure what you want to do over a lifetime, let's find out what you're going to do the remainder of this year.

Let's try to set our goal up a little higher than average and not too far in the distance. If you're in a business, a profession, or a job, your definite major purpose could enable you to step up your income from whatever your services may be now.

Then, at the end of the year, you can review your record and reestablish your definite major purpose and step it up into something bigger to another one-year plan or maybe to a five-year plan.

The starting point of personal initiative is to find out where you're going, why, what you're going to get out of it financially. I really believe the clear majority of individuals in the world can become very successful if they will just make up their mind on how much success they want and in what terms they want to evaluate success.

Many individuals want a good position and plenty of money but they're just not quite sure what kind of position or how much money they want or when they want to get the money. Let's do a little thinking on that subject and grade us on number one.

2. **An adequate motive to inspire continuous action in pursuit of the object of one's definite major purpose is to start studying yourself and see if you have an adequate motive or motives.**

It will be very much better if you have more than one motive for wanting to attain the object of your definite major purpose or your immediate purpose. Nobody ever does things without a motive and normal people move only on motive. We really don't have to have much brains to be very brilliant or have such a wonderful education to be an outstanding success.

We just need to take the little we have and start using it and putting it into operation and that calls for personal initiative.

3. A friendly mastermind alliance

This means friendly cooperation through which you can acquire the necessary power for noteworthy achievement. Take the personal initiative and see how many friends you can call upon if you were in the need of something in the way of cooperation.

If you need an endorsement or an introduction, or maybe you need a loan of money, unless you do have all the money you need just lying around, wouldn't it be nice to know somebody you could turn to for a favor, and get the money you need?

If you're aiming at anything above mediocrity, you will need at least one mastermind alliance with someone beside yourself who will not only cooperate with you, but who will go out of his or her way to assist you. It's up to you to take the personal initiative to build that mastermind alliance.

These people won't join you because you're a good-looking person. You will need a plan or have an objective, and you will need to find the individual or individuals suitable to make up your master-mind alliance. Then you will have to give them an adequate motive for them to become a mastermind ally of yours.

Don't be afraid to grade yourself zero on this one, but the next time you come back to this chapter don't grade zero. Grade much higher.

4. Self-reliance in proportion to the nature of your definite major purpose.

To check yourself on self-reliance, you may need help from other people. You may need some help from your wife or husband, or somebody who knows you well.

You may think you have self-reliance. Do you how to check yourself on self-reliance, and check it accurately?

Go back up to number one and carefully evaluate your definite major purpose. See how big that is in your life.

If you don't have a definite major purpose or if you do, and it's not anything outstanding above anything you have ever attained up to the present. Then, you do not have much self-reliance. If you have the proper amount of self-reliance, you will set your definite major purpose up way beyond anything you have ever achieved. You will then become self-determined to achieve that definite major purpose.

5. **Self-discipline sufficient to ensure mastery of the head and the heart to sustain one's motives until they are realized.**

When and where will you need self-discipline the most?

When the elevator reaches the top, and everything is going well and you're succeeding? You will need self-discipline when the going is hard, and the outlook is not favorable.

You will need self-discipline over your mind to the extent you know where you're going. You know you have a right to go there, and you know you're going to keep determined to get there regardless of how hard the going may be or how much opposition you may face.

You will need at least enough self-discipline to sustain you through the period when the going is hard instead of quitting or complaining.

6. **Persistence based on the will to win**

How many times does the average person has to fail before they quit or decide to do something else? Have you ever heard of the person who fails before they start, because they believe there's no use starting, thinking they can't do a thing? That cuts it down below one.

Then if people start, at the first opposition they meet they quit or allow themselves to be diverted into something else.

Can you guess what my outstanding asset happens to be? I have persistence and the will to win and the self-discipline to stick to a thing all the harder when the going is the hardest. That's my outstanding quality and always has been and always will be the remainder of my life. Without that trait, I couldn't have completed this book in my lifetime.

What about that trait? Is this something you're born with, or something you can acquire? You can acquire it, and it's not very difficult to acquire.

What causes a person to be persistent? A burning desire behind a motive is what makes an individual persistent.

I never think of persistence and a burning desire, and not think of my courtship. I don't think you can get very far in a courtship without being persistent. Don't you think that maybe you could transmute that emotion over into putting it behind your business or your job?

You must have just as much emotional feeling about attaining success in your job as you could about be selling yourself to the man or woman of your own choice.

If you don't know what the word "transmute" means, look it up, and if you haven't tried it, start trying it. The very next time when you feel moody or discouraged, try to change that over into an emotion of courage and faith, and see the great thing that happens to your personality.

It will change the whole chemistry of your brain,

and your body and brain become much more effective, whatever you're doing.

7. A well-developed faculty of the imagination controlled and directed

How important is an imagination controlled and directed?

An imagination not controlled and directed might become very dangerous for you.

I once worked for the Department of Corrections, and many of the men were in there, because they had too much imagination, and it was not controlled and directed in a constructive direction.

Imagination is a great thing, but if you don't have it under control and don't direct it in constructive direction, it may become very dangerous to you and a crutch for your freedom.

8. The habit of forming definite and prompt decisions.

Do you have the habit of forming definite and prompt decisions when you have all the facts at hand with which to make decisions?

If you do not have the habit of making decisions promptly and clear-cut decisions when all the facts are in, then you're loafing on the job. You're procrastinating and destroying that vital thing called personal initiative.

One of the finest places to start practicing personal initiative is to learn to make decisions firmly and quickly once you have all the facts.

I'm not talking about snap judgments, opinions, or snap judgments based upon half-baked evidence. I'm talking about all the facts on a given subject which are in your hands and available.

Then you should do something with those facts, make up your mind exactly what you're going to do, and not dilly-dally around, as so many people do in life. If you get into that habit of dilly-dallying around with everything, you will not be a person who acts upon his or her own personal initiative.

9.   The habit of basing opinions on guesswork instead of relying on facts

I wonder if you recognize how importance it is making it your business to get at the facts before you form an opinion about anything? Did you know you should never have an opinion about anything at any time, unless it's based upon facts, or what you believe to be actual provable facts?

Why is that true? Shouldn't you do that? You don't want to get into trouble, and you don't want to fail, do you? Of course, we can all go ahead and have opinions, and we all may have a flock of them.

We can even give them to someone else without their asking for them, and we do that right along. Before you can really and safely express an opinion or have one, you must do a certain amount of research and base your opinion upon facts, or what you believe to be actual provable facts.

10. The capacity to generate enthusiasm at will and control it

What happens before you start doing anything relating to your enthusiasm? You must feel the emotion, and your mind must be alerted with some definite objective, purpose, or motive. Then you will have to start doing something about that motive by words, facial expression, or some sort of action.

The word "action" is inseparable from the word "enthusiasm." There's passive enthusiasm which is something you feel but give no expression of it whatsoever. There are times when you need that kind.

If you don't, then you will disclose to other people what goes on in your mind at times when you don't want that to happen.

You take any great leader, or executive, and they may have a tremendous amount of enthusiasm.

They will display that enthusiasm only to whomsoever they please and under what circumstances they please.

They will not just turn it on and off, and leave it on like you and I do, or do we?

Controlled enthusiasm is enthusiasm turned on at the right time and then turned off at the right time.

Your personal initiative is the only thing that can control your enthusiasm.

If you take that one subject to turn on and off your enthusiasm and got the art down pat, did you know you could become a great salesman of anything you might ever want to sell?

Did you ever hear of anybody selling anything they didn't feel enthusiastic about what they were trying to sell or do for the other person? Did you ever sell anything you didn't have that feeling of enthusiasm over what you were trying to do for the other person?

If you didn't have that feeling of enthusiasm on your own personal initiative, then you didn't make a sale. Somebody may have bought something from you because they needed it or had to have it. You had very little to do with it unless, you imparted to them enthusiasm.

How do you impart the feeling of enthusiasm to another person when you're selling? You must be sold on it yourself, and it starts inside your own emotional makeup, and you must feel that way.

When you speak, you must speak with enthusiasm, and put on a good broad smile, because nobody speaks with enthusiasm with a frown on his or her face. There are many things you can learn about expressing enthusiasm and make the most of your enthusiasm. All of them involve your own personal initiative.

I can give you the component parts of enthusiasm

and how to express enthusiasm. The job of expressing it is up to the individual.

11. Tolerance

Are you open-minded on all subjects with all people always?

I'm open-minded on a lot of subjects I want to be open-minded on, but I shouldn't be. We shouldn't have any kind of attitude toward anybody else under any circumstance unless we can base that attitude upon something to justify that attitude or what we believe can justify that attitude.

Have you any idea how much value you deprive yourself all through life because you close your mind against somebody you don't like? That person might be the most beneficial person to you in the whole world?

Did you know one of the costliest things in an industrial or a business organization is the closed minds of the people that work there? If you didn't know that, I want you to find it out.

When you speak of intolerance, you might often think of somebody who doesn't like the other person, because of his or her brand of religion or politics. That really doesn't scratch the surface of the real meaning of the subject of intolerance. It extends to almost every human relationship.

Unless you form the habit of maintaining an open

mind on all subjects toward all people always, you can never become a great thinker or develop a great magnetic personality.

Did you know being close-minded causes you to not be very well-liked by other people? Do you know you can be very frank with people you don't like?

You can if these people know you are sincere in what you're saying, and you're speaking with an open mind.

The one thing other people will not tolerate is to recognize they are talking to somebody whose mind is already closed and what they're saying has no effect whatsoever regardless of how much value or how much truth there is to it.

Some individuals in the world have minds so definitely closed on so many subjects you couldn't get an ounce of truth in them if you lived a thousand years.

12. The habit of doing more than you're paid for all the time

This one you will have to move on your own personal initiative because nobody's going to tell you to do more or expect you to do more than you're paid for doing.

You don't have to ask anybody for the privilege for doing more than you're paid for doing.

If you start following this habit daily, sooner or later the law of increasing returns will begin to pile up dividends for you. When these dividends come back, they will come back greatly multiplied.

13. Tactfulness in speech and a keen sense of diplomacy

Are you tactful in your ordinary conversations with other people?

What about being tactful with other people, do you think it's worth the time it takes to be tactful? You always get the cooperation from others much more easily if you're tactful.

If you told me you've got to do something, I might say, "Well, you just hold on a minute, maybe I must do something," but if you put it to me like that, I'm going to set up some resistance right away.

If you would say to me, "I would very much appreciate it if you would do something for me," and you had the right to demand that from me, then there would be no resistance.

One of the most impressive things I learned in my research was Andrew Carnegie never commanded anybody to do anything. No matter who that person was, he requested that person to do something. He never commanded them. He always asked them if they would mind doing a certain thing, or say please.

It's surprising the amount of loyalty Mr. Carnegie had from his mastermind alliance. They'd go out of their way for him anytime of the day or night because of his tactfulness in dealing with them.

When it was necessary for him to discipline any one of them, he usually invited them out to the house and gave them a nice steak dinner or a five-or six-course dinner.

After the dinner was over, the showdown came when they went into the library, and Mr. Carnegie would start asking them questions.

One of his chief secretaries was scheduled to become a member of his mastermind group, and this boy found out he was scheduled for a big promotion. The seed was planted in his head, and he commenced to run around with a bunch of high bidders who threw cocktail parties. This boy's eyes were hanging out on his cheeks when he would come into work every morning.

Mr. Carnegie let that go on for several months and then the young man got invited out to the house one evening to eat dinner. After the dinner was over, they went into the library.

Mr. Carnegie said, "Now, I'm sitting over there in your chair, and you're sitting over here in my chair.

I want to know what you would do if you were in my place, you had a man scheduled for an important promotion, and suddenly it seemed to have gone to his head. He started running around with fast company and staying out late at night, drinking too much liquor and paying too much attention to everything except his job."

The young man said, "Mr. Carnegie, I know you're going to fire me, so you might just as well start in and get it over with."

Mr. Carnegie said, "Oh, no, if I wanted to fire you, I wouldn't have given you a nice dinner and invited you out to my house. I'm not going to fire you, I'm just going to have you ask yourself a question and see whether you're able to fire yourself. Maybe you're closer to it than you realize."

The young man did an about-face and did become a part of Mr. Carnegie's mastermind group and a millionaire later.

That young man absolutely saved himself from himself.

Mr. Carnegie's tactfulness was out of this world. He knew how to handle individuals and how to get people to examine themselves. Self-analysis is one of the most important forms of personal initiative anybody can possibly engage in.

I never let a day go by when I don't examine myself to see where I fall and where I'm weak. How I can make improvements, and what I can do to render more service and better service? I examine myself every day. I can always find someplace where I can improve. I can always find ways of doing something better and something more. That's a very healthy form of personal initiative. It gets very interesting because you finally get down to where you'll be honest with yourself.

The kind of personal initiative to help you find your weak spots is the kind of personal initiative most people won't engage in, because it involves self-analysis and self-criticism. Then you can be kind of confidential about it, can't you? You don't have to publicize these weaknesses when you find them out. Some of them you can get corrected before anybody else finds out about them, if you do a good job. If you must wait until somebody else calls them to your attention, then they may become public property, and they may embarrass you. They may hurt your pride, or even cause you to build up an inferiority complex when the other person must point out your weaknesses to you.

That's personal initiative, too, in finding out what your weak spots are, and what has caused you to be disliked by other people. It might be why you're not getting ahead as well as some of these other people when you know you have just as much brains or even more brains than they have.

Another great place to take personal initiative is to compare yourself with other people who are succeeding beyond your success. Make comparisons and analyses to see what it is they have that you don't have, and you'll be surprised to find out how much you can learn from the other person.

Maybe you can learn from the person you don't really like very well because if they are doing better than you're doing, believe me, you can always learn something from them.

Sometimes you can learn something from the person who is not doing as well as you, because it works both ways, and you may find out why they're not doing as well.

15. The habit of listening much and talking only when necessary

Have you ever heard of anybody learning anything while they were talking?

Maybe they might learn not to talk so much, and this seems funny, but it's not funny, it's very serious.

Most kids today do a lot more talking than they do listening.

They seem so dead bent on getting the other person told off instead of listening to see what the other person has to say that they might profit by.

16. A well-developed sense of observation of details

Can you walk down the main street in your hometown and, when you get to the end of the block, give a very accurate description of everything you've seen in every window?

Mr. Napoleon Hill once belonged to a class in Philadelphia directed by a man who was teaching the importance of observation of small details.

He said it was the little details that made up the successes and the failures of life and not the big ones. The ones we usually pass aside as not being very important or we don't even observe.

As part of the training, the instructor took them out from the study hall down the hall from the classroom outside of the building to the street.

Then they crossed over the street to the other side and walked up the street one block.

Then they crossed back over the street and they came back down the street one block.

Then back inside the building and walked down the hall back into the study hall.

In doing so, they passed about ten stores, one of which was a hardware store window.

In that hardware store's window there were easily five hundred articles.

The instructor asked each one of them to take a pad of paper and a pencil along giving them a crutch for their memory and to put down the things they saw as they passed that they thought were important.

Guess what was the greatest number of things any of them wrote down? Going one block one way, then a block down the other side of the street covering at least twenty stores.

The greatest number of things anybody had down was fifty-six.

When one man came back he didn't have any paper or pencil.

He listed 746 and described each one of them and told what window it was in and what part of the window it was in.

Mr. Hill didn't accept it and he had to go down after the class was over and backtrack to double-check it.

He was absolutely 100 percent accurate.

This man trained himself to observe all details and not just a few of them but all of them.

A good executive, a good leader, a good anything is an individual who observes everything that's happening around them.

They observe all the good things and all the bad things.

They observe all the positive things and of all the negative things.

They don't just happen to notice the things that interest them.

They happen to notice everything that may interest them or may affect their interest.

17. The capacity to withstand criticism without resentment.

One of the finest things that can happen to any individual is to have a regular source of friendly criticism of the thing that constitutes one's definite major purpose.

I invite it because the things you're doing daily might be offending other people, and you think they are all right, or else you wouldn't be doing them.

You're going to keep on doing them if somebody doesn't call them to your attention, isn't that right?

So, you need to have a source of friendly criticism, and

it's one of the most marvelous things in the entire world.

I'm not talking about the people who don't like you, and they criticize you just because they don't like you.

On the other hand, I wouldn't pay too much attention to the person who gives me friendly criticism just because they love me.

Out in Hollywood when those stars begin to believe the press agents and sometimes they do, they're just about through.

We all need to have the privilege of looking at ourselves through the eyes of other people.

I'll assure you when you walk down the street, you won't look the same to the other person as you think you look to yourself.

When you open your mouth, and speak in conversation or otherwise what registers in the other person's mind is not always registering what you think it is registering at all.

We all need people to point out changes as we go along because if we didn't, we would not grow.

Did you know many people resent any kind of suggestion or criticism that differs from what they are doing?

Anything that would change their way of thinking or their way of doing things, they resent it, and consequently these people do themselves very great damage by resenting constructive criticism.

I think there is such a thing as constructive criticism.

I want you to remember that no matter who you are or what you're doing or how well you do it, you might never get 100 percent approval from the crowd.

Don't expect it and don't be too disturbed if you don't get 100 percent approval. Just stay positive.

18. Loyalty to all to whom loyalty is due

I would place loyalty at the top of the list in my book of rules of qualifications of the people I want to be associated with all the time.

If you don't have loyalty to the people who have a right to your loyalty, then you might just as well have nothing.

No matter how brilliant you are or how sharp you are or how smart you are or how well educated you may be. The smarter you are, the more dangerous you may be if you don't have loyalty.

If you don't have loyalty, then maybe you can think of the person in connection to which you don't have loyalty and maybe you can decide to do something about being loyal.

I have loyalty to all people.

I do have a sense of obligation to them, if I'm related to them in business or in the profession or in the family circle.

There are a few people in the family circle I don't

particularly get along with, but I'm loyal to them.

I have that obligation.

If the members of my family want to be loyal to me, that's great.

If they don't, then that's their misfortune, not mine.

I have the privilege of being loyal, and I'm going to live up to that privilege.

Because of the values I get out of being loyal.

I must live with this fellow.

I must sleep with him.

I must look at him in the mirror and shave his face.

I must give him a bath occasionally.

I must be on good terms with him.

You can't live that closely with a fellow and not be on good terms with him.

"To thine own self be true, and it must follow as the night the day thou canst not than be false to any man." Shakespeare never wrote anything more beautiful and more philosophical.

If you're loyal to yourself then chances are you will be loyal to your friends and to your business associates.

19. The necessary attractiveness of personality to induce cooperation

Is an attractive personality something you're born with or something you can acquire on your own personal initiative?

You can acquire an attractive personality.

There's only one trait of these twenty-five factors that go into making up an attractive personality you're not born with, and that's personal magnetism.

You could even do something about that one because every one of these twenty-five factors are subject to cultivation through your own personal initiative.

First, you've got to know where you stand on each one of these points, and you can't always take your own word about your personality.

You've got to get your wife or your husband or friend or somebody else to grade you on your personality.

Sometimes these enemies will tell you where you fall, and did you know these enemies are good things to have occasionally?

Why?

They don't pull punches.

If you will examine what your enemies or those who don't like you say about you, the chances are you might learn something of value.

If nothing else, you'll learn at least you'll see to it that you don't let them tell the truth.

Don't be afraid of the people who don't like you.

They may say things that will put you on the track of discovery of something you need to know about yourself and your personality.

You can do something about your personality and find out what traits irritate other people.

You can even correct those traits.

You will have to first make the discovery yourself or you will have to get somebody who is frank enough to do it for you on that subject.

20. The capacity to concentrate your full attention upon one subject at a time

When you make a point, do you exploit it right down to its final analysis and then make a climax and get on to your next point?

Do you try to cover too many points at one time?

If you do that, you will not cover any points at all.

Grade yourself on the capacity to concentrate full attention upon one subject at a time.

If you're doing ordinary conversation or speaking or thinking or writing or teaching or whatever you're doing in life.

You should concentrate on one thing at a time.

21. The habit of learning from your mistakes

We must learn from our mistakes, or we just might as well not make any of them.

Have you ever seen a man duplicating a mistake repeatedly?

Remember the old Chinese aphorism: "Fool me once

shame on the man. Fool me twice shame on me."

22. A willingness to accept full responsibility for the mistakes of your subordinates

If you have subordinates and your subordinates make mistakes, it's you who have failed and not the subordinates.

Train them to do the thing right or put them in some other job where you won't have to supervise them.

Let somebody else do that.

The responsibility is yours if the person working under you is subordinate to you.

23. The habit of adequately recognizing the merits and abilities of others

Don't try to steal the thunder from the other person.

After they had done a good job.

Give them full credit and give them more rather than less.

A little pat on the back has never been known to hurt anybody when you know they have done a great job.

The more-successful people like recognition.

Sometimes individuals will work harder for recognition than they do for anything else.

There was a book written that was widely distributed all over this country, and the central theme was if you want to get along in the world, flatter people.

Flattery is as old as the world, and one of the most costly and deadly weapons and the most dangerous.

I like people to compliment.

If someone came up to me and said, "Mr. West, I appreciate what you're doing for our country.

Would you mind if I came around to your house later tonight, so I can talk to you about a business proposition?"

I'd say they have flattered me in order that they may get some of my time and some benefits from me.

24. The habit of applying the Golden Rule principle in all human relationships.

One of the finest things you can do for yourself is to always put yourself in the other person's position.

When you go to make any decision, or engage in any transaction involving any other person, you should always put yourself in their position.

If you do that, you'll always do the fair thing to the other person.

25. The habit of assuming full responsibility for any task you have undertaken

Did you know the one thing most individuals are most adept in doing is creating a reason they didn't succeed or why they didn't get the job done right?

If many individuals who create alibis would put in half as much time in doing the thing right or trying to do it right than they do putting into explanation why they didn't do things right.

They'd get a lot further in life and become much more successful.

The person who is the cleverest at creating alibis is the most inefficient person in the whole works.

They make a profession of spinning alibis and make them up in advance.

When these people are called on the carpet or get caught over the barrel, they have an answer.

There's only one thing that counts, and that's success.

Napoleon Hill once wrote an epigram covering this subject that effective.

"Success requires no explanations, failure permits no alibis.

If it's a success, you don't need any explanations.

If it's a failure, then all the alibis and all the explanations in the world won't do any good because it's still a failure, isn't it?

26. The habit of keeping your mind occupied with what you desire and not that which you don't desire

In the clear majority of instances in which most people engage in personal initiative is regarding the things they don't want in life.

Here is one place where most people don't have to

be taught to take their personal initiative on that subject.

That's precisely what you get out of life.

The things you think about and the things you attune your mind to in life.

Here's a little place where the word transmute can come into play.

Instead of thinking about the things you don't want and all the things you fear or distrust or dislike.

Start thinking about all the things you like.

All the things you want.

All the things you're going to become determined to get.

There is no defeat except from within.

There is really no insurmountable barrier save your own inherent weakness of purpose.

— EMERSON

7

A POSITIVE MENTAL ATTITUDE

In this chapter you will learn how to whip the seven basic fears in life.

For reference, they are:

1. The fear of poverty
2. The fear of criticism
3. The fear of ill health
4. The fear of the loss of love
5. The fear of old age
6. The fear of the loss of liberty
7. The fear of death

Nothing constructive and worthy of man's efforts ever has been achieved or will ever be achieved except that which comes from a positive mental attitude.

A positive mental attitude backed by a definite major purpose and that definite major purpose activated into an intense burning desire until that burning desire is elevated to the plane of applied faith.

There are four different states of the mind or levels

or conditions of the mind that all lead up to a positive mental attitude.

Condition level one: Wishes

Wishes we all have a stock of wishes.

A wish for this and a wish for that and a wish for a lot of things.

Nothing very much happens when you just wish for things in life does it?

No nothing happens.

Then you go a little bit further, and you become curious by putting in a lot of time through idle curiosity.

Do you think anything happens with idle curiosities?

No, nothing really happens with idle curiosity.

However, we can and do consume up a lot of your time

With idle curiosity, don't you?

You put in a lot of our time studying what your neighbors do or do not do.

You spend a lot of time studying what your competitors do or do not do just out of idle curiosity.

That's not leading to a positive mental attitude.

Condition level two: Hope

Now, your wishes have become hopes of achievement, hopes of attainment, hopes of accomplishment, and hopes of accumulation of things you desire.

But just a hope by itself is not very effective because we all have a flock of hopes.

Not all of us who have hope have success, we just hope for success.

It is better than wishing for it.

What is the difference between a hope and a wish?

A hope is beginning to take on the nature of applied faith isn't it?

That's the idea.

You're transmuting a wish into that very desirable state of mind known as applied faith.

Condition level three: Burning Desire

Now, you've stepped up your positive mental attitude to where your hopes are becoming transmuted into something more known as a burning desire.

Is there any difference between an ordinary desire and a burning desire for things?

A burning desire is an intensified desire based upon hope of a definite major purpose.

How does one go about developing a burning desire for anything?

You can't do it without having a burning desire or one of the nine basic motives behind your definite major purpose, can you?

The more motives you can have for a definite thing, the more you can fan your emotions up quicker into what is known as a burning desire.

There's another state of mind we must have before you can make sure of your success.

Condition level four: Applied Faith

Now you've transmuted wishes, idle curiosity, hopes, and even a burning desire into something still higher and that is applied faith.

What's the difference between applied faith and ordinary belief in things?

That word applied might just as well be synonymous to action.

You can say active faith and applied faith mean the exact same thing.

A prayer only brings positive results only when it's expressed in a positive mental attitude.

The most effective prayers are the one's expressed by the individual who has conditioned their mind to habitually think in terms of a positive mental attitude.

Did you know even the most successful individuals in the world spend a large amount of their time each day in negative thinking?

The very outstanding successes in the world the

great leaders are the ones who put in very little time thinking about the negative side of life.

They put all their time thinking on the positive side.

Mr. Hill once asked Henry Ford if there was anything in the world that he wanted, or that he wanted to do that he couldn't do.

Mr. Ford said, "Why, no, I don't believe there was." Mr. Hill then asked Mr. Ford if there ever had been, and Mr. Ford said, "Oh, yes, back in the early days before I learned how to use my mind."

Mr. Hill asked Mr. Ford, "Now just what do you mean by that?"

Mr. Ford said, "When I want a thing, or want to do a thing, I start in finding out what I can do about it. When I start doing that I don't bother about what I can't do because I just let that alone."

That was his only statement, but I want to tell you there's a world of philosophy wrapped up into that statement.

Mr. Ford put his mind on doing something about the part he could do something about. I venture the suggestion if you put a difficult problem to most people. These people will immediately begin to tell you why the problem can't be solved. If there is anything about the problem that is favorable and anything about the problem that is unfavorable, most people will see the unfavorable side first, and oftentimes never see the favorable side to the problem.

I can't think of a single problem that could confront me that wouldn't have a favorable side to the problem. If nothing else, the favorable side would consist of the fact if it's a problem I can solve, I will solve it. If it's a problem I can't solve, I will not worry about the problem.

Most individuals when confronted with a difficult problem they can't solve start worrying. Then you go into what state of mind? A negative state of mind, and do you ever accomplish anything worthwhile while you are in a negative state of mind? No, you're only muddying the water when you have a negative mind. You must learn to keep your mind positive when you want to do things that are worthwhile.

Does a negative mental attitude attract favorable opportunities for you or repel them? It repels them, doesn't it? Does the repelling of those opportunities have anything to do with your merit or with your right to have opportunities? Nothing whatsoever, because you may have all the right to have all the good things. If you're negative, you will repel all those great opportunities leading to the attainment of those great blessings. So, your job mainly is to keep your mind positive, so it attracts to you all the things you want and all the things you desire.

Have you ever stopped to think why prayer generally doesn't bring anything except a negative result?

I believe that's it's the biggest stumbling block to most people in all religions. These people don't understand why prayer brings a negative result or generally brings a negative result. You couldn't expect anything else because there's a law that governs that in life.

The law is your mind attracts to you the counterpart of the things that the mind is feeding upon. There are no exceptions for anybody. If you want to attract what you desire through prayer, you must believe. But, you must put action behind that belief, and transmute that belief into applied faith.

You can't have applied faith in a negative state of mind because the two just don't go together. There is a method by which one may transmute failure into success, poverty into riches, sorrow into joy, and fear into faith. The transmutation procedure is simple. It starts with a positive mental attitude, because success, riches, and faith do not make bedfellows with a negative state of mind.

You can very well afford to come back to this chapter many times, assimilate it, and make it your own.

When failure overtakes you, start thinking what would have happened if it had been a success instead of a failure.

Then start looking for the seed of an equivalent benefit that comes with every adversity, defeat, and failure.

Do you think that's difficult to do? No, it's not difficult at all. Every adversity, failure, and defeat have a seed of an equivalent benefit when you go searching for that seed.

When poverty threatens to catch up with you or has caught up with you, start thinking of it as riches, and visualize all the riches in all the things you would wish to do with actual riches.

I remember when I was a little boy. I ran away from home one afternoon. I didn't want to do my chores.

I knew I was going to get beat with the belt when my parents arrived home. I rode my bicycle down to the Arkansas River. As I was sitting down on the bank of the Arkansas River in Great Bend, Kansas, it was getting dark, and I was starting to get hungry. I started to look around for ways to catch a fish to eat. I finally got so tired of looking for ways to catch a fish, I shut my eyes for a few moments.

I considered the future and saw myself going away becoming a rich and famous racecar driver, then one day returning home to that very spot. I had built myself up into a state of ecstasy in that time of poverty, need, want, and hunger. Maybe, I've kept those hopes alive. Maybe my writing this book and keeping my hopes alive will bring me that "Great Personal Power" race car and race team.

I want you to start looking forward and imagining the things you desire and transmuting unfavorable circumstances into something that's pleasant. By that I mean start switching your thoughts away from thinking about unpleasant things over onto something that is pleasant. When fear overtakes you, just remember fear is only your applied faith in reverse gear. Start thinking in terms of faith as seeing yourself translating your faith into whatever circumstance or thing you desire.

I don't think anybody ever escapes experiencing the seven basic fears at one time or another in their life.

If you allow fear to take possession of you, it will grip you and become a habit with you. It will certainly attract to you all the things that you don't want in your life. You must learn to deal with fear by transmuting, converting, or transferring it over in your mind to something the opposite of fear, in other words, faith.

If you fear poverty, just commence to thinking of your-self in terms of opulence and of money. Start thinking of all the ways and means you're going to earn and acquire that money. Start thinking about what you're going to do with the money after you get the money. There's no end to the daydreaming you can do. It's far better to daydream about the money you're going to have than to fear the poverty you know you already have. There is no virtues and no benefits in sitting down and bemoaning the fact you don't have any money and you don't know how to get the money.

I honestly believe there isn't anything in the world

that money or anything else can buy that I can't get if I want to get it. I don't think in terms of what I can't get. I think in terms of what I can get. I've been doing that for a long time.

It's a great thing to condition your mind so you're more positive. Then when any emergency arises, you have the habit of a positive mental action. You can't get a positive mental attitude by just wishing for one. You get it by weaving a cord of a rope day by day a little bit at a time.

My invisible guides to riches

I want you to create in your imagination an army of invisible guides, counselors, or mentors who will take care of all your needs and desires. If you understand metaphysics, you might say this is a fantastic system I have worked out for myself. It is a fantastic system because it looks after all my needs and all my wants.

I fully realize these guides, mentors, or counselors are the creation of my own imagination. I'm not trying to kid myself, you, or anybody else. For all practical purposes, they represent real entities and real people. Each one is performing the exact duty I assigned to them and doing it all the time.

The guide to physical sound health

Did you know a strong physical body is the temple of the mind? It must be sound. There must be plenty of energy.

When you turn on the old enthusiasm button, if there's no energy, you can't generate something out of nothing.

I don't know how anybody can express intense enthusiasm when the body is in a series of aches and pains.

So, your first duty to yourself should be for your physical body to see that it responds to all your needs. It does for you all the things your body is supposed to do every day.

You need a little bit more help than what you get in the day.

When you lay your body down each night to sleep, nature goes to work on your body and gives you a tune-up and a working over of your body parts. You must have that trained entity called the guide to sound physical health. That guide supervises your health and makes sure it does its job properly.

The guide to financial prosperity

How can anybody be of any great service to others or race cars without money? How long can you get along without money? You've got to have money. You must have a money consciousness.

That entity you're building up through that guide gives you money consciousness. My guide is so controlled that if he doesn't make any money, I won't permit that to happen.

I won't permit myself to become too greedy or pay too much for the money I earn.

I know some people who paid too much and died too young trying to get too much money. They put too much effort into accumulating money they didn't need or couldn't use.

It's my guides business to see that I stop when I do get enough. This is a philosophy dealing with economic success.

Success wouldn't consist of destroying yourself and dying too young because you tried to get too much of anything in life. Stop when you get enough. Make better use of the things you have right now instead of trying to get more things you're not going to make any use of at all.

Remember the wonderful statement that comes out of the Bible? I won't translate it verbatim. The meaning of it is not too much and not too little of anything. (Proverbs 30:8, 9) That's one of the blessings of this philosophy: it gives you a balanced life. You learn what is enough and what is too much.

The guide to peace of mind:

Why is peace of mind so important? What good is it if you owned everything in the world, and you could collect a royalty from every person without peace of mind? I'm emphasizing this point here, my friend, because I've had the privilege of doing the research and studying the most outstanding and richest men our country ever produced.

Mr. Hill has taught me the importance of learning to live a balanced life.

So, as you go along you can have peace of mind. You can make your occupation or your daily labor a game you get great joy from doing, not something to be a burden or dreaded. It can be a game you would play as ardently as a person playing a game of golf, tennis, basketball, or some other game you love. When a man or a woman gets in a position where he or she can do a thing for the sake of love, I want to tell you they're really very fortunate. This philosophy leads to that very condition. You can never attain that position until you learn to maintain a positive mental attitude at least a major portion of your time.

One of the saddest things I learned during my research was Mr. Carnegie didn't have peace of mind. In his latter years Mr. Hill said Mr. Carnegie practically lost his mind trying to find ways and means of disgorging himself of his fortune. Mr. Carnegie's major obsession in this part of his life was to get this philosophy well-organized while he was living and in the hands of other people. Mr. Carnegie wanted to provide people with the know-how of success by which people could acquire material things, including money, without violating the rights of other people.

It would have been a great joy and quite enough compensation for a lifetime of effort and work if I could have met those wonderful men in person. I would want to thank them for directing me in my life when I needed direction. I'm not so sure they're not looking over my shoulder right now.

I do things beyond my reasonable intelligence. The things I do which might be called brilliant or outstanding are always done by the men looking over my shoulder.

In the time of any emergency when I must make an important decision, I can almost feel those men telling me what decision to make. I can turn around and imagine them looking over my shoulder in person. It's as good a time as any for me to tell you. I could have never done what has been done about this book if it wasn't for the men who helped me do it. I don't want people feeling I have been favored, or I have anything you can't have.

I think whatever source of inspiration I'm drawing upon, is just as available to you as to me or anybody else. I believe that with all my heart.

The Guide to Hope and Faith

These two guides of hope and faith are twins. You must have that eternal flame of hope and faith, or there wouldn't be anything worth living for. You can develop a system for keeping your mind positive, because there are so many things to destroy hope and faith, like people and circumstances that you can't control that pop up. You must have a system in place to counteract those things and to offset them with something you can manipulate and draw from.

The guide to love and romance:

These next two guides to love and romance are also twins.

I don't believe anything worthwhile can be accomplished unless a man or a woman romanticized whatever they are doing. If there's no love in your heart, then you're not quite a human being.

Love and romance are great builders of geniuses, leaders, and maintainers sound health. To have the great capacity to love has been the privilege of rubbing elbows with geniuses. These two guides, love and romance, in my life their job is to keep me friendly with what I'm doing. They not only keep me young in body and mind, they keep me enthusiastic and sold on what I'm doing.

I recognize before you get in a position where you can economically forget about earning a living, there are some things you might have to think about that may take a little bit of the pleasure out of your work.

Learn to get love and romance into your life and to cultivate a system where love and romance will express themselves in everything you want to do every day.

The guide to overall wisdom:

The guide to wisdom is the controller of the other seven.

His business is to keep them active, and eternally engaged in your service, to adjust yourself to every circumstance, pleasant or unpleasant, so you can profit by every circumstance.

I can tell you nothing comes to my mill that isn't grist.

I make grist out of everything that comes to my mill.

The more unpleasant things that come to my mill, the more grist I get out of them. I doubly grind them to make sure they won't be anything else but grist.

Did you know you can always profit by every experience if you have a system for profiting? If you let your emotions run wild and go down under the unpleasant experiences, you will attract more unpleasant experiences than you will pleasant ones.

There's a peculiar thing about unpleasant circumstances.

They're cowardly. When you get them by the horns and you say, "Come on over here, little fellow, I've got a harness right here, and I'm going to put you to work."

Somehow or another they find business around the corner, and they don't come your way as often as when they know you're going to put them to work.

If you fear unpleasant circumstances, they'll crowd down on you in flocks. They will come in through the back and come in the front door. They will come in when you're not expecting them to come in or when you're unprepared to deal with them. I don't particularly invite unpleasant circumstances. If they're foolish enough to come my way, they'll find themselves ground up in my mill of life. I'll make grist out of them as sure as anything. I will not go down under them.

Eternal vigilance is the price one must pay to maintain a positive mental attitude because of other natural opposites of positive thinking.

Did you know there are negative entities working inside your physical makeup all the time, constantly maneuvering to gain power over you on the negative side? You must be eternally on the alert to see that those negative entities don't take you over. Then your accumulated fears, self-doubts, and self-imposed limitations you will have to deal with constantly lest they get the upper hand, and they become the dominating influence in your mind.

Beware of these negative influences near you, including people who are negative, whether the people you work with closest, the people you live with, or maybe some of your own relatives who are negative. If you don't watch out, you'll be just like they are, because you'll respond in kind.

It may be necessary for you to live in the same

house with somebody who is negative. It's not necessary for you to be negative just because you are in the same house with someone who is negative. I'll admit it can be a little bit difficult to immunize yourself against that kind of influence, but you can do it.

I have done it; Mr. Hill has done it; Mahatma Gandhi did it. Look what he did with immunizing himself against the things he didn't want in his life.

Perhaps some inborn negative traits you brought over with you from birth can be transmuted into positive traits as soon as you find out what they are in your life. I'm quite convinced there are a lot of people who are born with natural traits of a negative nature.

You take a person who was born in the environment in poverty. All his relatives are poverty stricken. All the neighbors are poverty stricken. He saw nothing but poverty and felt nothing but poverty and heard nothing but poverty talk. That was the condition I was born in.

I know you can be born with that kind of negative trait.

That was one of the most difficult things I had to whip, the inborn fear of poverty along with worrying over the lack of money and lack of progress in your business or professional calling. You can put in most of your time in worrying over these things or you can transmute your state of mind over into working out ways and means of overcoming these worries. Worrying over the negative side is not going to do anything except get you in deeper and deeper and deeper; that's all it's going to keep doing.

You don't have to let these unrequited and unpleasant love affairs destroy your balance of mind, as so many people do.

It's up to you to maintain a positive mental attitude.

Recognize your first duty is to yourself. Start getting control of yourself, and don't allow anybody, emotionally or otherwise, upset your equilibrium. Watch your unsound health, whether it's real or imaginary. You can worry an awfully lot about health by worrying about things you think might happen to you but never do. Your mental attitude has a tremendous amount to do with what happens to your physical body.

You think you weren't feeling very well. Let some good piece of news come along, and see how quickly you snap out of the sick feeling you were experiencing. Then, the lack of an open mind on all subjects with all people at all times causes much trouble to many people maintaining a negative mental attitude. Don't get into the habit of allowing other people to do your thinking. These are the prices you must pay and the things you must concur with to have a positive mental attitude.

Then the ignorance of the real extent of the power of your own mind and its unlimited potential for the attainment of anything you desire can come into play.

Only the lack of a definite major purpose and a definite philosophy by which to live and guide your life will hinder you.

Did you know the majority of people in the world have no philosophy? They live by hook or crook, by chance, or by circumstance. They're just like a dry leaf on the bosom of the wind. They go whichever way the wind blows. There's nothing they can do about it, because they have no book of rules to go by and trust luck and misfortune.

Generally, misfortune rules. You must have a philosophy you can live by.

That's what you're reading in this book. It's a philosophy you can live by in such a way your neighbors around you look upon you as someone desirable. They feel happy to have you there. You feel happy to be there. You not only enjoy prosperity, contentment, and peace of mind, you also reflect that in everybody you come into contact with.

That's the way people should live life. Everyone desires to be rich, but not everyone knows what constitutes enduring great riches.

Here are the twelve great riches:

I want you to familiarize yourself with them, because before anybody can become truly rich, they will need to have a fairly well-balanced proportion of all these twelve great riches.

There are eleven other things more important than money, if you're going to have a well-rounded and well-balanced life:

- A positive mental attitude
- Sound physical health
- Harmony in human relations
- Freedom from fear
- Hope of future achievement
- Capacity for applied faith
- Willingness to share one's blessings
- Engaged in a labor of love
- An open mind on all subjects toward all people
- Complete self-discipline
- Wisdom with which to understand people
- Money to top it all off

When a man really finds himself at the top of the ladder of success, he is never alone, because no man can climb to genuine success without taking others with him.

8

SELF-DISCIPLINE

This "Challenge to Life" essay is a brilliant essay Mr. Hill wrote. I want to share with you, because this essay really helped me respond in a positive way during one of the worst defeats I've ever had in my entire life. I want to bring this essay to your attention to give you an idea of how I go about transmuting any unpleasant circumstance into something useful when this circumstance happened to me. I had real reason to go out and fight. I don't mean fight mentally or fight orally I mean fight physically.

If I had to settle the matter from behind an oak tree with a machine gun, it would have been justified under the circumstance. Instead of doing that, I elected to do something that would do no damage to anybody else and would benefit me. I elected to express my pain, sorrow, and defeat through this wonderful essay.

A Challenge to Life

Life, you can't subdue me, because I refuse to take your hardships too seriously. When you try to hurt

John West

me, I laugh, and the laughter knows no pain.

I appreciate your joys wherever I find them. Your sorrows neither discourage nor frighten me, for there is laughter in my soul. Temporary defeat does not make me sad; I simply set music to the words of defeat, and turn it into a song. All your tears are not for me; I like laughter much better, and because I like it much better, I use it as a substitute for grief, sorrow, pain, and disappointment.

Life, you're a fickle trickster; don't deny it. You slipped this emotion of love into my heart so that you might use it as a thorn with which to prick my soul, but I have learned to dodge your trap with laughter. You try to lure me with a desire for gold, but I have fooled you by following the trail that leads to knowledge instead. You induce me to build beautiful friendships then convert my friends into enemies, so you may harden my heart. But, I have sidestepped your fickleness by laughing off your attempt and selecting new friends in my own way.

You cause men to cheat me at trade, so I will become distrustful. But I win again, because I possess one precious asset, which no man can steal. It is the power to think my own thoughts and to be myself. You threaten me with death, but to me death is nothing worse than a long, peaceful sleep, and sleep is the sweetest of all human experiences except laughter. You build the fire of hope in my heart, and then sprinkle water on the flames, but I do something better by rekindling the fire, and laugh at you once more. Life, you are licked as far as I am concerned, because you have nothing with which to lure me away from laughter, and you are powerless to scare me into submission. To a life of laughter, I raise my cup of cheer.

I want you to know it was not very easy for me to express myself through an essay about an unpleasant experience where you have been damaged, hurt, and injured by those who should have been loyal to you.

This business of striking back at the people who have injured you or the people who have tried to injure you is just a lack of your self-discipline. You haven't really become acquainted with your own "Great Personal Power", and your ways and means of benefiting by that "Great Personal Power." Don't stoop to the low level of trying to strike back at another person who has slandered you or vilified you or cheated you in one way or the other in life. Don't ever strike back at them because you will only lower yourself in your own estimation and that of your Creator.

There's a better weapon I'm trying to place into your hands, so you can defend yourself against anyone that would injure you.

I hope you will take my word for it. Use the self-discipline based on this chapter, and never allow anybody drag you down to his or her level. You set the level you want to deal with people, and if they want to come up to your level, well, all right; and if they don't, let them stay down on their level because there's no sin in doing that in life. Set your own high level and stand your ground come what may, because you have a better way of defending yourself. You have a mind and you know how to use that mind. You're never without any defense.

Auto-suggestion or self-suggestion

Auto-suggestion or self-suggestion is suggestion to self through which dominating thoughts and deeds are conveyed to the subconscious mind. The medium and the starting point in the development of self-discipline is a definite major purpose.

You'll notice in each one these chapters you can't get away from the term "definite major purpose", because it stands out like a sore thumb, and because it's the starting point of all achievement.

What do you think is the reason for repetition of an idea?

Why should you write out your definite major purpose,then memorize it and go over it day in and day out as a ritual? To get it into the subconscious mind because the subconscious mind gets into the habit of believing what it hears repeatedly.

You can tell the mind a lie repeatedly, and you'll finally get to where you don't know whether it's a lie or not. It's funny, but it happens to be true. I know a lot of people who have done that very thing their whole life.

How do you create a burning desire for anything?

You can do it by writing down your desires or goals, reading them daily, calling it into your mind, and seeing the physical manifestation of them somewhere in the circumstances of your own life.

You have a burning desire to buy a new car while you're driving a used one. You don't have enough money in the bank to get it. What can you do? Every time you get into your old car and just before you turn the key, you shut your eyes for a few moments and imagine yourself sitting in a nice, brand new car.

Then you imagine yourself purring down the street in the old one as you give her some gas and imagine yourself owning that nice new car. You don't exactly have possession of it yet, but for the time being, you're there at the wheel of your nice new car. It may sound silly, but I talked myself into a newer BMW that very way.

I used to drive an older model BMW and wanted a new one. I found a BMW car agency that had the exact one I had pictured in my mind, even down to the aluminum wheels. I called the car salesman and spoke with him on the phone, describing the car I was looking to buy. The car salesman said he would have to check my credit and call me back. When he called me back, he said, "Mr. West, come on down. I have the car ready for you to test-drive."

I got into my old BMW and drove down to the car dealership.

He had the new BMW ready for a test drive and he handed me the keys. He did show me a little trick or two I needed to know about a newer BMW to get the best results out of them. We drove down Highway 680 in Concord a little bit, and we both got out of the car, and he shook my hand. He said, "Mr. West, I'm very happy to have the privilege of selling you this nice car."

Be careful before you set your heart upon something through a burning desire, because the subconscious mind goes to work translating that burning desire into its material equivalent. The reason it's important for you to be careful about what you set your heart upon is you're going to get it. Just make sure it's something or someone you will be willing to live with the rest of your life.

While I was doing my research, all the people I dealt with were immensely wealthy. I didn't pay attention to any other kind people. I was only interested in the ones who had made a big demonstration financially. You might be interested in knowing every single one of them had an abundance of wealth. Not all of them had peace of mind. They neglected to balance themselves along with their wealth, so it wasn't such a burden to them. To me, the most pitiful sight for me to see in the world is an extremely rich man or woman who doesn't have anything else but monetary riches.

The next most pitiful sight for me to see is a boy or girl who has come into monetary riches without earning them. The power of thought is the only thing which any human being has complete unchallenged right of control over, and it's controlled by the power of the will. God chose the control of our thoughts to be one of the most important of all gifts. This is a stupendous fact which merits your most profound consideration. If you give it this sort of consideration, you will discover for yourself the rich promises available to those who become master of their mind power through self-discipline.

Self-discipline leads to peace of mind and harmony within one's own mind. I could not tell you I have everything I could possibly need, I could possibly use, or I could possibly wish for in the world of abundance. I got it through self-discipline.

There was a time when I had much more money in the bank. I wasn't as rich then. I'm very rich today, because I have a balanced mind. I have no grudges; I have no fears; I have no worries. I learned through self-discipline to balance my books with life. I have a big boy up somewhere that stands looking over my shoulder that I'm at peace with all the time. I couldn't be at peace with him if I hadn't learned the art of self-discipline.

I am learning how to respond to these unpleasant things of life in a positive way instead of in a negative way in my life.

I'm not sure what I would do if someone walked up to me on the street and slapped my face real hard.

I'm still human. I might just double up my fist and hit them right in the nose. I would if I was put in the position to defend myself. I would just take a few seconds to think before I did something like that to someone. I would just pity them for being such a fool as to do a thing like that to me.

There are some things I used to do the wrong way. I have learned how to do them in the right way through self-discipline. I'm in a position today to be at peace with all people. If you're not at peace with yourself and at peace with these people you work with every day. Then you're not rich. You will never be rich until you learn through self-discipline to be at peace with all people.

I have Catholics and Protestants, Jews and Gentiles, and people of different colors, races, and creeds reading this book. To me everyone is the same color and the same religion. I don't know the difference, and I don't want to know the difference. In my mind there is no such a thing as a difference.

Do you know one of the curses of this world in which we're living, and particularly here in this melting pot of America, is that we haven't learned how to live with one another? We are in the process of learning. When we are all indoctrinated with this philosophy, we'll have a better world here in the United States of America.

Self-discipline enables one to keep the mind fixed on the things which are wanted and off the things which one does not want.

If this philosophy doesn't do anything else for you except start you on a habit or a plan whereby you can occupy your mind from here on out, mostly with the things you desire. Then keep your mind off the things you don't desire. Then, all the time and money you spent on this book would be paid back a thousand times over.

You will experience a new birth, a new opportunity, a new life.

You just learn through self-discipline to not let your mind feed upon the miseries, the disappointments, or the people who injure you. I know what I'm telling you to do is much easier for me to tell you than it is for you to keep your mind mostly occupied with the money you're going to have. I'm not unappreciative of such a difficult thing it is for you to keep your mind mostly occupied with the money you're going to have when you might not have any right now.

I know all about not having money. I know what it is to be hungry. I know what it is to be without a home and without friends. I know how difficult it is when you're illiterate, ignorant, or poverty-stricken, and to think in terms of becoming an outstanding philosopher, spreading your influence all throughout the world. I know all about it, but I did it. I'm speaking in the past tense. I did it. I know if I can conquer the things I have conquered in my life, then I know you can do a good job. I want you to keep your mind so busy and occupied with the things you want and with the people you like. You will have no time left to think about the things you don't want and the people that you don't like.

Speaking about the people you don't like, have you ever thought of examining very carefully as near as you can without being biased against these people you think you don't like? Don't look for their faults and justify your opinion of them. That's the natural thing to do; that's what the weakling would do. If you're a strong person, you will look fairly and squarely, and you will find some good things in every human being.

There is nobody in the world so very bad they don't have any good qualities in them. If you never look for the good things, you will never find any good things. I think it's one of the evils of this age in which we're living; maybe it's the evil of all ages.

When we encounter other people, if they give us the slightest reason, we not only look for all their shortcomings but we multiply those shortcomings by stepping them up into something bigger than they really are. That's really a great discredit and a great disservice to the person who does it.

You can under-evaluate your enemies to where they'll destroy you. You can also underestimate your opposition, too. You will have opposition, but you can convert that opposition from enemies into friends. You will have to start working on yourself and become charitable, understanding, and forgiving.

If a person does do you an out-and-out injury without any provocation, you have one of the grandest opportunities in the world to do what? You have the prerogative right to forgive them and pity them, don't you?

I want to emphasize my three mental walls of protection I have against outside forces. This system works like a charm for me.

When you get to where you have so many wonderful friends all over the world, you will need a system for how many of them you can see in a given time. You won't have to have one in the beginning. I didn't have one in the beginning, but I do today. I have this system of a series of three imaginary walls. They're not so imaginary. They are pretty real.

The first one is a rather wide wall. It extends way out from me, and it's not too high. It's high enough to stop anybody who wants to get over the wall and get to me, unless they give me a very good reason for me to see them. They have to go through some formality. Why do I have this wall, and just leave it down? It's because my wonderful friends all over the world would take up much of my time. I can reach millions of them dealing with me through my book. When they want to see me in person, I have to have a system. Then, when people get over the first wall, they immediately meet another wall.

That wall is not so big and not so commodious, but it's many times higher. People can't go over that wall with any stepladder. I'll tip you off on how you can do it. If you have something I want, you can get over that wall and get to me very easily. But I must be convinced the time I devote to you will be of mutual benefit to both you and me.

Then, when you get over the second wall, you come to another wall. This wall is very much narrower, and it's as high as eternity. No living person gets over that wall. There is where I do my best work.

When I began to write this book, I retired into my sanctuary.

I communed with my Maker. I got instructions. When I come to an intersection in my life, and I don't understand which way to go or if I should go back or ahead, I always asked for guidance. I always got that guidance. Don't you see how wonderful it is to have a system of immunity for yourself, and how unselfish it is? Your first duty is to yourself. Remember Shakespeare's marvelous poetic lines?

"To thine own self be true, and it must follow as night the day thou canst not than be false to any man."

When I first read that, I started repeating it, and I have repeated it a thousand times because of how true it is. Be true to yourself: protect your mind, and your inner consciousness. Use your self-discipline. Take control of your own mind, and direct your mind to the things you want most and desire. That's one of the most important and precious gifts from the Creator to mankind.

I want you to make up a list of five traits of your personality you think you need self-discipline to improve. If you can't think of any, get your wife to tell you. Maybe your husband will do a good job. In some cases, you won't even have to ask your husband, because he'll tell you without it, or the wife vice versa.

Just for the sake of doing an experiment, right now, mentally what is your first one? After you do discover any defects in your personality, ones that you may need to improve through self-discipline, you should put them down on paper. That will help you, start immediately to develop the opposite of those traits.

If you're in the habit of not sharing your opportunities or your blessings with other people, start sharing. If you're in the habit of being greedy or anything of that sort, start sharing. If you've been in the habit of passing on a little gossip, stop passing out gossip, and start passing out complimentary things. Why, you would be surprised. You would see a person blossom like they have never blossomed before. That person will be a different person if you start telling them the good things about themselves, and not the bad. Don't rub it on too thick, because they'll wonder what you're after.

Anytime somebody walks up to me, shakes my hand, and says, "Mr. West, I appreciate so much the book you have written,"

I just want to tell them, I have found myself. I'm a success in my profession or in my business, and I owe it to the philosophy of "Great Personal Power". I know that person is telling the truth, because of the tone of their voice, the look in their eyes, and the way they take hold of my hand. I appreciate that kind of a complimentary remark.

If they stood there and rubbed it on too thick, out of proportion of what I deserved, then I would know right away they were getting ready for a touch of some sort. You do have to use discretion in all these things.

Then, after you've made up your list of all these traits of a pleasing personality you believe you need to improve by self-discipline, I want you to make up one for your mate that you believe needs self-discipline for improvement. I want you to observe the difference as to the ease with which you can carry out that transaction compared to the one where you're looking into your own traits of character that need to be improved by self-discipline.

Self-examination is a very difficult thing for everyone, because we are all biased in our favor. We think whatever we do, no matter how it turns out, if we did it, then it must be right. If it doesn't turn out right, it was always the other person's fault.

Someday I'm going to have the experience of somebody telling me they have been at odds with somebody for a long time.

Then, when they started applying this philosophy in their life, the trouble was not with the other person; it was with them.

They started to improve themselves through self-discipline, and when they got their own house clean, the other person's house was also clean. That's the way it will work out.

It's very astounding as to how many motes you can see in the other person's eye when you're not looking for those in your own eye. I think before anyone starts to condemn anybody, they should stand in front of a mirror and look themselves in their eyes to find out if they have clean hands. When that's made into a practice, you can get to the point at which you can forgive people for almost anything.

What is the most important form of self-discipline which should be exercised by all who aspire to outstanding success?

There's only one. It's the control of your thoughts. As a matter of fact, there's nothing else of more importance in the entire world than the control of your own mind. If you control your own mind, you will control everything you come into contact with throughout life. You will never be mastered by circumstances. You will never be the master of the space that you occupy in the world, until you first learn to be the master of your own mind.

Mahatma Gandhi, in biding his time to gain freedom for India, used these four principles:

A definite major purpose – He knew what he wanted.

Applied faith – He began to do something about it by talking to his fellow men and indoctrinating them with the same desire. He didn't do anything vicious, and he didn't commit any acts of mayhem or murder.

Mastermind Alliance – Gandhi went the extra mile and formed a mastermind alliance which this world had never seen before with at least two hundred million of his fellow men and women. These all contributed to that mastermind alliance, the main object being to free themselves from England without violence.

Self-discipline – Gandhi practiced self-discipline on a great scale without parallel in modern times.

These are the elements that made Mahatma Gandhi the master of the great British Empire.

Where in the world would you find a man who would stand all the things that Gandhi stood? All the insults and all the incarcerations he faced? He still stood his ground but did not strike back in kind. Mr. Gandhi struck back, but it was on his own ground and with his own weapons.

When you go to battle, select your own battleground and your own weapons. Then, if you don't win, it's your own fault. I want you to remember that throughout life. You're going to have to do battle one way or another in life. You will have to plan your campaigns to remove opposition from your way.

You've got to be smarter than your opposition and your enemies. The way to do that is not to strike back on battle grounds of their choice and with weapons of their choice.

Select your own weapons and select your own battle ground.

Condition yourself first for the battle by making up your mind you're not under any circumstance going to try to destroy anybody or to do anybody any injury other than that of defending your own God-given rights. When you take that kind of positive mental attitude, you're going to win before you start.

I don't care who your opposition is, or how strong or smart they are, you're bound to win. Your reward for using that God-given brain is mastery of your own destiny through the guidance of infinite intelligence.

Reward for what? Taking control over your own mind. It gives you direct contact with infinite intelligence. There is no doubt about that in the whole world. When I tell you there's a person standing looking over my shoulder guiding me, I particularly tell you the truth when I meet with any obstacles, all I have to do is remember He's right there.

If I come into an intersection in my life, and I don't know which way to turn, this way or that way, go ahead or go back, all I have to do is remember I have an invisible force looking over my shoulder. He will always point me in the right direction if I have faith and pay attention to Him.

How would I know that's true? I can only know that by my own experience, practicing it and dealing less with theory. I'm not going to be guilty of telling you anything will happen unless I have made it happened, and I tell you how you can make it happen.

The penalty one must pay for not taking full control of your own mind is the penalty most people will pay all through their life. You will become the victim of the stray winds of circumstances, which will remain forever beyond your control. What do I mean stray winds of circumstance? You become the victim of every influence you come into contact with. All those enemies and things you don't want will sway you like a leaf on the bosom of the wind.

Isn't it a profound thing to recognize the truth? You have been given a means by which you can declare and determine your own earthly destiny. Then, along with it comes a tremendous reward you automatically receive if you just accept and use that great asset. If I didn't have any other evidence of a first cause or of a Creator than what I know about that principle, I would have to know there had to be a first cause. That's just too profound for any human being to think up, giving a man or woman a great asset and rewarding them for accepting it and then penalizing them for not accepting it.

That's the sum and substance of what happens to

you when use your self-discipline and take full control of your own mind.

Direct your mind to the things you want. Never mind what you want; that's nobody's business but yours. I don't want you to ever forget that in life. Don't let someone come along and sell you the idea as to what you should want. Who's going tell me what I want or what I should want?

That's right. It hasn't always been like that, but it's like that today. There isn't anybody going tell me what I want or what I should want if I would allow anyone else to do my thinking,

I think it would be an insult to my Creator. He intended that I should have the last word about this guy. Believe me, I'll take the last word.

I would do nothing in this world under any circumstance to hurt, injure, or harm a single human being. Did you know whatever you do to or for another person, you do to or for yourself? That's an eternal law.

I'm proud of myself I didn't follow my inclination to become a divorce attorney while going through my divorce. I got a firsthand view of what it's like to be on the bad side of domestic relations trying to get custody of my son. My ex–wife had all her friends write inaccurate information about me. I was humiliated in front of the judge. That would make the judge believe I wasn't a very good father, and I would lose custody of my son. I did lose custody of my son. I was being judged by snap judgments, which is a common trait of all of us. We judge people by the ones we know best. It's not fair to do that to people, certainly not in my case.

I want to bring to your attention some of these things you will need to deal with. You will need to learn to understand yourself and learn to understand how to adjust yourself to other people who are very difficult to get along with. We can't do away with the people, but we can do something by doing something with ourselves. That doesn't mean changing your mind or your body. It means controlling your mind and body.

The great emotion of sex gets more people into trouble than all the other emotions combined. It's not the emotion that gets people in trouble; it's their lack of control of that emotion and directing it or transmuting it.

So, it is with the other faculties of the body and the mind.

It's not that you must change completely; it's just you must be the master in control. You must recognize the things you need to do to have sound health and peace of mind. It means you will not accept or submit to the influence of any circumstance or thing you do not desire.

You may have to tolerate the circumstance, and you may have to recognize it's there. You don't have to let these circumstances conquer you, because you are going to assert that you're stronger than the circumstance. You can give your imagination a wide range of operation as to what these things are in your life. I won't mention any of them because they may be too personal. It means you will build a three-wall protection around yourself, so no one will ever know all about you or what goes on in your mind.

J. Edgar Hoover, with whom Mr. Hill had done some professional work on great many occasions, said the persons he's investigating are the best help to him of all. Mr. Hoover said he got more information from the person he was tracing than from all other sources combined.

Mr. Hill asked why, and Mr. Hoover said, "Because he talks too damn much."

Tell me what a man fears, and I will tell you how to master him.

If I wanted to control anybody, it would be only on the basis of love and under no other basis.

You need have no fear of competition from the person who says, "I'm not paid to do this, and I will not do it." They will never be a dangerous competitor for your job. But watch out for the person who remains at their work until it is finished and performs a little more than expected of them, for they may challenge you at the post and pass you at the grandstand.

9

ENTHUSIASM

The starting point in creating enthusiasm is based upon a burning desire. When you have learned how to work yourself up into a state of a burning desire, you won't need the rest of the instructions on enthusiasm because you've already got the last word in enthusiasm.

When you desire something really badly, and you make up your mind to get the thing you desire, you have that burning desire, and it steps up your thinking processes, and starts your imagination to go to work in finding out ways and means of your getting the thing you desire. That enthusiasm gives you a brighter mind and makes you more alert to opportunities you have never seen before when your mind is stepped up into a state of enthusiasm for something definite.

There is active enthusiasm and passive enthusiasm. The active enthusiasm is more effective. What do you think I mean when I say "active and passive enthusiasm"? I'll give you an illustration of passive enthusiasm.

Henry Ford was the most lacking in active enthusiasm of any man Mr. Hill ever met in his life. Mr. Hill never did see him laugh but once. When Mr. Hill shook hands with Mr. Ford, it was like taking hold of a piece of cold ham.

You did all the shaking. Mr. Ford did nothing but stick his hand out and take his hand back when you let go of his hand.

In Mr. Ford's conversation, there was no magnetism in his voice, and no evidence in any shape, form, or fashion of his demonstrating active enthusiasm. Mr. Ford must have had some to have such an outstanding definite major purpose and to achieve it so successfully. Mr. Ford's enthusiasm was transmuted into his own imagination, his own power of faith, and his own personal initiative. Mr. Ford went ahead on his own personal initiative. Mr. Ford believed he could do whatever he wanted to do. Mr. Ford kept himself alert and keen with his applied faith through his passive enthusiasm and thinking inside of his own mind what it was he was going to do and all the joy he'd get out of doing it.

This was long after Mr. Ford had arrived and had his problems whipped.

Mr. Hill once asked Mr. Ford if he ever wanted anything or wanted to do anything that he couldn't do. Mr. Ford said, "No," and then he qualified himself, "Not in recent years."

In the early days until he learned how to do or how to get whatever it was he wanted, he couldn't answer in the affirmative. Mr. Hill asked, "Well, then, Mr. Ford, there isn't anything you want or need that you can't get?"

"That's right, that's correct."

"How do you know that's true? How do you go about making sure whatever you're going to do you know you're going to do it before you start?"

"Well, for a long time I've formed the habit of putting my mind on the can-do part of every problem. If I have a problem there's always something I can do about the problem. There are many things I can't do, but there are some things I can do. I start where I can do something.

As I use up the can-do part of the problem the no can-do part simply just vanishes. When I get to the river where I expected to need a bridge I didn't need the bridge because the river was dry."

Isn't that a great statement for a man like that to make?

Mr. Ford started in on his problem or in on his objective in life where he could do something. Mr. Ford said if he wanted to turn out a new model, or if he wanted to increase his production, he immediately put his mind to work on the plan to which he could do something, and he never paid any attention to any obstacles. He knew that his plan was sufficiently strong and definite, backed up with the right kind of applied faith that the opposition he might meet with would melt away when he came to it.

Mr. Ford said, "The astounding thing was if you took that kind of mental attitude of putting your mind behind the can-do part of every problem, the no-can-do part simply just takes to its heels and runs."

I can endorse everything Mr. Ford said because that's been my experience. My experience has been if you want to do something, you'll work yourself up into a white heat of enthusiasm and go to work right where you stand. If it's nothing more than drawing a picture in your mind of the thing you want to accomplish, then keep drawing that picture and making it more vivid all the time.

If you start with the tools that are available to you now, and then other and better tools will be placed in your hands.

Teachers and speakers express enthusiasm by the control of their voice.

I want to share a personal story with you: One day one of my friends asked me if I had any teaching or public speaking experience or voice training. I said, "No, not a thing." The answer to my voice is no matter who hears it or how much a cynic the person is, the person knows one thing - I believe what I'm saying; I'm very sincere about what I'm saying to them.

This is one of the best things I know anything about is expressing yourself in terms of belief in the thing you're saying at the time is the thing you ought to say, and it will do some good to the other person and perhaps some good for you, too. This enthusiasm is a great tool for any negative influence that might get inside of your mind. If you want to burn up a negative influence, just turn on old enthusiasm; the two can't stay in the same room at the same time.

Naturally you'll start changing your tone of voice, and you'll go out deliberately intending to make some person smile while you're talking to them and make that person like you more. You should start observing these people who do express enthusiasm in their conversational relationships. I like to see a person soften up their face with a smile while they're talking to me.

You'll get a great lesson on attractiveness of personality by studying people. If you see a person you particularly like, start watching them, and find out what makes you like them. The chances are a thousand to one you'll find out in whatever conversation the person engages in it will be on an enthusiastic basis. You'll never get bored no matter what they say or how much they say.

You can learn to express your enthusiasm by practicing in front of a mirror and talking to yourself in the beginning if you can't find anybody else willing to listen to you. Be sure and always say the things you want to hear when you start talking to yourself in front of the mirror.

I stood before a mirror for the last fourteen years. I told myself, "Now look here, John West, you really admire Napoleon Hill's style of writing, the clarity, the succinctness, the definiteness, the simplicity of the language. John West, you really admire Napoleon Hill, but one day you're going to catch up with him." I did just that by talking to this fellow and convincing him it could be done.

Be sure to close the bathroom door, and don't leave the door open very wide if there are people around. These people will call the psychiatric ward and divorce you if you're married. Really and truly we all need to do an overhauling job on us at one time or another.

I want to attain a greater degree of proficiency all the time.

My education is never completed. It's wide open all the time. As long as you're green, you'll continue to grow.

But, when you get to where you're ripe with all knowledge, then the next step is to become rotten.

I'll never be ripe with all knowledge and never learn the last word about anything. I'm always learning from other people, but I wouldn't learn anything without an open mind.

When you express enthusiasm in your daily conversations, observe with profit how others pick up your enthusiasm and reflect it back to you as their own. You can change the attitude of anybody you want to by simply working yourself up into a state of enthusiasm. That's a contagious thing, and other people pick it right up and reflect it back to you as their own.

All master salesmen understand the art of how to key up the buyer with their enthusiasm. That works just the same in selling yourself as it does in selling services, commodities, or merchandise. You go into any store and pick out a salesman who knows his or her business, and you'll recognize right away that the salesman or saleswoman not only sells you merchandise, but along with it will give you information in a tone of voice that's really impressive.

Anytime I go into a store and somebody with a pleasing personality helps me, I always seem to end up leaving the store with more than I really needed, so I'm not immune to salesmanship.

You know there are a lot of people in the world who allow the death of a loved one to run them distracted. I've known people who lose their minds over a death. When my mother-in-law passed away, I knew she was going to pass away because of her medical condition. I knew it was only a question of time. I had conditioned my mind so that it would not possibly upset me or make the slightest impression on me emotionally. I didn't show any expression of sorrow of any kind. What was the use? I couldn't save her; she was dead. Why grieve myself to death over something I can't do anything about?

You might think that's hardhearted, but it's not at all.

I knew it was going to happen. I had adjusted myself, so it would not destroy my confidence or make me afraid. Did you know when you're upset emotionally you're not quite sane, and you don't digest your food? You're not happy, and you're not as successful. Things go against you when you're in that frame of mind.

I don't want things to go against me. I want to be healthy, and I want to be successful. I want things to come my way, and the only way I can insure that is to not let anything upset any one of my emotions.

I don't think anybody can love any deeper or more often than I have loved. I didn't want my ex mother in-law to die.

As long as she was dead there wasn't anything I could do to save her life. That's an extreme illustration I'm giving you, but it's certainly one needed by everybody. We need to learn to adjust ourselves to the unpleasantness of life without going down under the unpleasant circumstances.

The only way to do that is by diverting your attention away from the unpleasant things over to something pleasant.

Remember from this day forward your duty to yourself requires you to do something each day to improve your technique for the expression of enthusiasm. When you meet with any sort of unpleasant circumstance, learn to transmute the unpleasant circumstance into a pleasant feeling by repeating your definite major purpose with great enthusiasm.

When anything unpleasant comes along in your path of life, instead of brooding over it or allowing it to take up all your time in regret or in frustration or in fear, just start switching your thoughts over to thinking about the marvelous thing you're going to accomplish one month, two months, six months, or one, two, three, four, or five years from now. Start using your enthusiasm for what you desire and have not lost through defeat.

Maybe, in your circumstances and considering your relationships with other people you know there is something you can do to start stepping up your enthusiasm to make yourself more beneficial to some other person.

If you have a mate, and you can work up the relationship to where the mate compliments you in every place where you're apt to be weak, then you've got a fortune you can't estimate and an asset beyond comparison with anything else in the world.

The mastermind relationship between a man and his wife can surmount and master all difficulties. They do it by multiplying and joining their positive mental attitudes with enthusiasm and by turning it on each other at the places where they are in need.

Singleness of purpose is one
of the chief essentials for success in your life
no matter what may be one's aim.

—*John D. Rockefeller, Jr.*

10

CONCENTRATION OR CONTROLLED ATTENTION

I never did find in my research a successful person in the upper brackets of success in any calling who hasn't acquired the great potential powers of concentration upon one thing at a time. You've heard other people speak of others intending it to be derogatory by calling them "people with one-track minds". Have you ever heard that term?

Anytime somebody says I have a one-track mind I must thank them, because there are a lot of people in the world who have multi-track minds, and they try to run on all of them at the same time.

I have observed the most outstanding successes of the world are the individuals who have developed a high capacity to keep their mind fixed upon one thing at a time.

When you have learned to concentrate on one thing at a time, you have learned how to key yourself up and see yourself in the possession of the thing you're concentrating on.

The nine basic motives are the starting point of all concentration.

Let's say you wanted a better job, so you can make more money to buy an estate. If you concentrated on money in the upper brackets, you would be surprised at how that concentration would change your whole habits of thinking, then attract to you opportunities for making money that you had never thought of before. I know because that's the way it worked out for me some years ago.

I wanted to buy a half million-dollar estate. I was concentrating on approximately $465,000 to get the estate I wanted. From the very first day I fixed in my mind the size of estate I wanted to acquire, opportunities began to develop for me to get that money. I got a job working for the Department of Corrections, and I sold myself on the idea I needed the money and was going to render service for the money. I did get the estate, but I wouldn't have gotten that estate if I hadn't concentrated on that idea.

When you put a burning desire behind a motive, it moves you into action and attracts you to others who might help you to fulfill that strong desire. How do you go about developing a strong desire or a burning desire about anything? Do you do it by thinking about a lot of different things and changing your mind from one thing to another?

No, you select one thing, and you eat it, sleep it, drink it, breathe it, and talk about it as long as you can find anybody willing to listen to you. You do it by repetition and keep telling your subconscious mind exactly what you desire. You make it clear, plain, definite, and above everything else, you keep telling yourself you expect results and no fooling. Then an organized endeavor or your personal initiative is the self-starter that starts the action behind your concentration. Then your applied faith is the sustaining force that keeps action moving in the right direction. Without that applied faith when the going gets to be hard, and it will not matter what you're doing, you might slow down or quit. So, you can see you will need applied faith to keep your action keyed up to a high degree even when the going gets hard, and it will not matter what you're doing.

Have you ever heard or seen anybody start out to do anything of an outstanding nature and achieving outstanding permanent success right from the start without any opposition? I'm going to tip you off on the fact that nobody has ever done that, and probably nobody ever will.

The going is always hard with everyone no matter what you're doing.

But, now you got a tremendous amount of information behind every one of these chapters to help you concentrate. You might have to come back to each chapter many, many times. You will have to concentrate on each chapter. While you're concentrating on a chapter, put everything else aside and concentrate on that chapter. Then add to your notes everything you can get related to that subject.

While your concentrating on a given chapter, don't let your mind run over all the other chapters. Stick right straight to that one chapter you're concentrating on. Then the mastermind alliance is the source of allied power necessary for you to ensure your success behind your concentration.

Can you imagine anybody concentrating on the attainment of something of an outstanding nature without making use of the mastermind, the brains, influence, and education of other people? Did you ever hear of somebody achieving outstanding permanent success without the cooperation of other people?

I'm going to tip you off. I have never found anybody in the upper brackets of achievement who didn't owe their success very largely to the friendly harmonious cooperation of other people, the use of other people's brains, and sometimes, other people's money. So, you will need to have a mastermind alliance in your concentration if you're aiming for anything above mediocrity.

Of course, you can do your own concentrating on failure.

You won't need any help on that, but you will have a lot of volunteer help and a lot of company along if you just aim to fail. If you're going to succeed, you've got to follow these regulations that I'm laying down for you to follow.

You can't escape any one of them, and you can't neglect any one of them.

Then, the chapter on self-discipline is the watchman that keeps your action moving in the right direction, even when the going does get difficult for you. There is where you need your self-discipline the most when you meet with any opposition, or you meet with any conditions that you've got to cut through that are very difficult. You will definitely need your self-discipline the most then to keep your applied faith going and to keep yourself determined that you're not going to quit just because the going does get hard for you.

So, you couldn't possibly get along in concentrating without self-discipline. You could if you had everything going your way, and you didn't meet any difficult circumstances or conditions that you've got to cut through.

Then, the chapter on creative vision and your imagination is the architect that fashions practical plans for your action behind your concentration. Before you can concentrate intelligently you must have a plan. You must have an architect. That architect is your imagination or the imagination of your mastermind allies if you have them.

What do you think can happen if you started out to do something without a definite or practical plan?

Did you ever hear or see somebody who had a very

fine objective, purpose, or idea, but it failed because they didn't have the right kind of a plan for putting it over? Isn't that a common pattern for somebody to have a good idea, but the plan for carrying out that good idea was not sound?

Then, going the extra mile is the principle that ensures harmonious cooperation from others. This is when you will need your concentration. If you're going to get other people to help or get them to do something, you have got to put them under obligation and give them a motive. Even your own mastermind allies in your own organization won't serve as a mastermind ally without a motive.

What is the most outstanding motive that would get someone to join you in a given undertaking? The desire for financial gain. In all business and professional undertakings, the desire for financial gain is the most outstanding motive. If you're going into a business where the main object is to make money, and you don't allow your mastermind allies, your key men or women, or the people who are helping you the most get sufficient returns, they'll be going into business for themselves, or they'll be going over to your competitors and what-not. Then, the applied Golden Rule gives you moral guidance to the action's effect on your concentrating.

Then, the chapter on accurate thinking saves you from daydreaming into the creation of your plans. Did you know most of the so-called thinking in the world is nothing but daydreaming, hoping, and wishing? There are many individuals in the world who spend the majority of their time daydreaming, hoping, wishing, and thinking about a lot of things, but never do take any actual physical or mental, concrete action in carrying out those plans.

Then the chapter on learning from adversity and defeat ensures one against quitting when the going gets hard.

Isn't it a great thing to know you've learned beyond any question of a doubt that failure, defeat, and adversity needn't stop you? There is always a seed of equivalent benefit in every such experience.

Can you see any benefit in a man's going through a divorce, losing his house and custody of his son, going through a bankruptcy, and then years later again losing another house and going through another bankruptcy, having to start all over twice while doing the research for this book? That was the greatest blessing that has ever came along in my life, because I was becoming a smartypants and had to get taken back a few notches.

I've made a comeback, and have performed more good work since that time. Adversity is a blessing in disguise, and oftentimes not so much disguised. If you take the right mental attitude towards the adversity, you can't be whipped out, and you can't be defeated until you have accepted defeat in your own mind.

I want you to always remember, no matter what the nature of your adversity is, there is always a seed of an equivalent benefit if you look for the good instead of the bad. Don't spend anytime brooding over the things you've lost or the mistakes you have made. Put in productive time analyzing, learning, and profiting from them, so you won't make the same mistake twice. You will see controlled attention involves the blending and the application of many of the principles of the philosophy. "Persistence" should be your watch word. Controlled attention is the twin brother of a definite major purpose.

Just think what you could do with those two principles.

You have a definite major purpose and know exactly what it is you want, then concentrate everything you got on carrying out that definite major purpose. Do you know what can happen to your mind, brain, and whole personality if you would concentrate on one definite thing?

What I mean by concentrating is doing it day in and day out, and in a little while you'll get to the point in every which way you turn you find something in the way of an opportunity that will lead you a little bit closer to the thing that represents your definite major purpose.

Take Henry Ford, for instance. We all know what his definite major purpose was, and most people have been driving his definite major purpose around every day of their lives. It was to make and distribute all over the world low-priced, dependable automobiles. Sticking to that job made Mr. Ford fabulously rich.

There were hundreds of men that came into that field and spent infinitely more money than Mr. Ford had to start out with, and these people went back into the graveyard of failure. There were men who were better educated than Mr. Ford. There were men who had better personalities than Mr. Ford. There were men who had a lot more except for one thing. They didn't stick to the one definite major purpose the way he did when the going was hard.

Mr. Edison, in the field of invention, was a marvelous illustration of what concentration can do. If you want to know the truth about Mr. Edison, if he was a genius in any sense, it was because when the going was hard, he turned on the most steam and didn't quit. Think of a man standing by and keeping on through ten thousand different failures as he did while he was working on the incandescent electric lamp. Can you imagine a man going through ten thousand failures in the same field without wondering if you shouldn't have your brain examined?

Mr. Hill saw Edison's logbooks, and there were two stacks of them. In each book were about 250 pages. On every page there was a different plan he had tried and had failed.

Mr. Hill asked, "Suppose you didn't find the answer. What would you be doing right now?"

"I would be in my laboratory working instead of out here fooling away my time with you."

Mr. Hill did say on his behalf he grinned when he said it, but believe me, I'm sure Mr. Edison meant exactly what he had said.

Infinite intelligence will throw itself on your side when it finds out you're not going to quit until it does. If you do not give up and quit when the going is hard, infinite intelligence will throw itself on your side. There you have your faith, your personal initiation, your enthusiasm, and your endurance tested. When nature finds out you can withstand the test and not take no for an answer, she says, "All right, you're over, you pass, you're in."

I think that nature or infinite intelligence or God or whatever you choose to call that first cause likes to convey information to people in simple terms they can understand.

Surely this philosophy comes into that category. This philosophy is designed so children of grade-school age can read and understand it. The moment you come into contact with each of these principles, your own intelligence tells you it's bound to be sound, and you can see its sound.

This philosophy wouldn't be in existence today if I hadn't concentrated through years of adversity and defeat. So, it does pay to concentrate, and my own experience collaborates what I just said.

If you stand by when the going is hard and fail to quit, infinite intelligence will throw itself on your side. That's not true with men such as Adolf Hitler, Saddam Hussein, Bin Laden, or any past dictators or men trying to divide nations. No doubt these men had a definite major purpose, and no doubt they had a burning desire. What was wrong with their definite major purpose? It ran counter to the plans of infinite intelligence. It ran counter to the laws of nature. It ran counter to the laws of right and wrong. You may be sure if whatever you're doing is wrong, you'll come to failure and grief if it works a hardship or an injustice upon a single individual. What you must do to have infinite intelligence throw itself on your side is to be right. The only way you can be right is when everything you do benefits everybody it affects, including yourself.

There is something in Mother Nature or infinite intelligence that brings forth every evil, the virus of its own destruction. There's no exception for anybody, because everything that's not in conjunction with the overall plan of nature or the natural laws of the universe brings with the circumstance itself the virus of destruction.

The signers of the Declaration of Independence, and George Washington, Abraham Lincoln, and Thomas Jefferson's concentration were to give personal liberties to all the American people of the world. This may be the cradle for the birth of the freedom of mankind. I know of no other nation on the face of this earth that is concentrating upon the freedom of the individual as we are doing here in the United States of America.

> *The only man who makes no mistakes*
> *is the man who never does anything.*
> *Do not be afraid of mistakes, providing*
> *you do not make the same one twice.*
>
> —*Roosevelt*

11

ACCURATE THINKING

Accurate thinking is an important principle that most people have never heard of, because this principle has never been taught in public schools. Accurate thinking is the ability to analyze facts, think clearly, and make decisions based upon accurate thinking instead of relying on emotions. The truth is most people around the world act upon feelings and their opinions, and do not make decisions based upon actual provable facts.

When it comes to a showdown between people's emotions and the things people's heads tell them about what they should do, which one do you think wins the most? Why doesn't the head or brain get a better chance or be consulted more?

There are certain simple rules and regulations to follow and apply to help avoid the common mistake of inaccurate thinking. What do I mean by the common mistake of inaccurate thinking? The common mistake is making snap judgments and being pushed around by your emotions. The truth is your emotions are not reliable at all.

Take the emotion of love. It's one the greatest and the grandest of all emotions, and yet the most dangerous by the same token. Perhaps more trouble and more difficulty in human relationships grow out of the misunderstanding of the emotion of love than from all other sources combined.

There are two kinds of thinking we do, and these are based upon three major fundamentals:

There's inductive reasoning based on assumption of unknown facts or hypotheses.

Then there's deductive reasoning based on the known facts, or what we believe to be the known facts.

Last, there's logic, and that's guidance by past experience similar to those under consideration.

These are the three types of thinking we do most.

Which one would you say we put into operation the most?

Inductive reasoning that is based on assumption of unknown facts or hypotheses is in operation most. That is where you assume you know the facts, but you really don't know the facts. You assume they exist, and you create opinions based on your judgment, not actual provable facts.

When you do that, you better keep your fingers crossed and to be ready to change your decision, because you're reasoning may not be accurate. You're basing your judgment upon assumed facts or opinions.

Then there is deductive reasoning. That is based upon known facts, or what is believed to be the known facts.

Deductive reasoning is when you have all the facts before you or in front of you. Then you can deduce from those facts certain things you ought to do for your benefit or to carry out your desires. That is supposed to be the type of reasoning or thinking many people engage in.

Only most people don't do a very good job of deductive reasoning.

There are two major steps in accurate thinking:

First:

The first step is separate facts from fiction or hearsay evidence. That's where you find out if you're dealing with facts or with fiction, real evidence or hearsay evidence.

If you're dealing with fiction or hearsay evidence, it behooves you to be exceptionally careful, keep an open mind, and not reach a final decision until you have examined those facts very carefully.

Second:

You should separate facts into two classes: important and unimportant.

What is an important fact? You'll be surprised when I tell you most facts people deal with on a day in and day out basis is relatively unimportant. I'm not talking about hearsay evidence or hypotheses. I'm talking about facts most people deal with on a day in and day out basis. Why? Let's see what an important fact is, and then you'll know why.

An important fact may be assumed to be any fact that can be used to the advantage in attaining one's definite major purpose or any subordinate desire leading towards the attainment of one's definite major purpose. That's what an important fact is.

I wouldn't miss it very much if I said many people spend more time on irrelevant facts that have nothing to do whatsoever with their advancement than they do on facts that would be of benefit to them. I'm talking about these curious people that meddle in other people's affairs, those who gossip, those who put in a lot of time thinking and talking about other people's affairs or dealing with petty small talk and petty facts.

If you doubt what I just stated is true, start taking inventory of the number of facts you deal with for just one whole day. Then sum up at the end of the day and see how many really important facts you have been dealing with.

It might be better for you to do this on an off day like a Saturday or Sunday or when you're away from your occupation or business, because that's when an idle mind usually goes to work on unimportant facts. Opinions are usually without value, because most opinions are based upon bias, prejudice, intolerance, guesswork, and hearsay evidence.

Then, all this free advice volunteered by friends, family, and acquaintances is usually not worthy of consideration.

Why? It's not based on facts and has too much small talk mixed in the free advice. The last part of the sentence is not meant to be funny.

What kind of advice is the most desirable advice when you need advice? How should one go about getting desirable advice? What kind of desirable advice should one recommended?

You should get advice from a specialist or recommended advice from a specialist who is known to be a specialist with the problem at hand. Then you will need to pay them for their service. You should never go to anyone for free advice. Why? Because free advice is just about worth what it costs. Everything in this wonderful world is just about worth what it costs.

What are love and friendship worth? Do they have any price? Have you ever tried to get love and friendship without paying the price and to see how far you go? Love and friendship are the only two things where you can't get the real McCoy unless you do give the real McCoy. If you try to mooch or try to get love and friendship without giving in return, your source of supply will soon play out.

Accurate thinkers permit no one to do their thinking for them. What do you think about that? How many people do you think permit circumstances, influences, radio, television, newspapers, and other people like relatives to do their thinking for them? What's the percentage of the people around the country do you think permit that? I wouldn't even want to make a guess, because it's very high, no fooling.

I have one asset that I really feel proudest to be blessed with. This asset is better than money, bank accounts, bonds and stocks, because it's something much more precious than all those things. What is it? I have learned to hear all evidence. Get all the facts I can find from all sources.

Then I put them together in my own way and have the last word in doing my own thinking. That does not mean I'm a know-it-all, a doubting Thomas, or don't seek any counsel. I certainly do seek counsel, but when I have gotten that counsel, I determine how much of it I will accept and how much of it I will reject.

When I make a decision, nobody in the entire world could ever say it wasn't a decision of John West, although it might be a decision based upon a mistake. It might be an error, but it's still mine, and nobody influenced me. That doesn't mean that I'm hard-hearted, and my friends have no influence on me. Certainly, they have an influence on me. But, I will determine how much influence they have on me, and what reaction I will have to their influence. I will never permit a friend to have such influence on me as to cause me to damage some other person just because that friend wants it done.

Doing your own thinking. I think the angels in heaven rejoice when they discover a man or a woman that does his or her own thinking and doesn't allow relatives, friends, enemies, and other people to discourage this business of accurate thinking. The reason I'm emphasizing the point along here, my friend, is that the majority of people never do take control of their own minds, the most valuable asset anybody has, the only one thing God gave to all of us, the only thing all human beings have complete control over.

But, the majority of people around this country generally don't discover or use it or allow other people to kick them around like a football. I'm not talking about you. I hope you do understand you're a friend of mine. I'm talking about "them", the ones who are not reading this book.

I don't know why in our educational system or somewhere in our system of teaching or writing that before now we haven't been informed that we have the greatest asset in the world. That asset consists of the privilege of using our own mind, thinking our own thoughts, and directing those thoughts into whatever objective we choose. Do you know why people don't do it? These people don't know they have it, because there has never been the proper system of education.

Whoever you see this philosophy touch, you start seeing people blossoming like they have never blossomed before.

It does make a difference, because people begin to find out they do have a mind, can use that mind, and make it do whatever it is they want it to do. I can't say everybody suddenly runs in and immediately starts taking control of his or her own mind.

These people rather sneak in or slip in a little bit at a time. Eventually, the affairs of people's lives begin to change, because they discover this great mind power and start using it.

It's not safe to form opinions based upon newspaper reports. "I see by the papers" is a preparatory remark usually branding the speaker as a snap judgment thinker. "I see by the papers", or "I hear tell", or "They say." How often have you heard those terms? When I hear anybody start off speaking like that, I mentally immediately put in my imaginary ear plugs. I don't hear a doggone thing that has been said. I know it's not worth hearing.

When anybody starts to give me information and identifies the source by saying, "I see by the papers" or "They say" or "I hear tell", I don't pay any attention to what is said whatsoever, not the slightest attention. Not that what they're saying might not be accurate. I know the source is faulty; therefore, the chances are the statement is also faulty. These scandalmongers and people who gossip are not reliable sources from which to procure facts on any subject whatsoever.

Why is that true?

They're not reliable; also, they're biased. Did you know when you hear anybody speak in a derogatory way about anybody else, whether you know the person or not, puts you on guard and gives you the responsibility of studying and analyzing very closely everything that is said, because you're listening to a biased person.

I think the human mind or brain is such a great wonderful thing. I really marvel at how smart the Creator was in creating a human being. Giving a human being all the equipment, machinery, and mechanisms to detect falsehood from truth is something present in the falsehood that notifies the listener of the statement. You can tell it, and you can feel it. Also, by the same token, when someone is speaking truth, the most finished actor in the whole world couldn't deceive you if you would use your innate intelligence in reference to these statements that are made.

Now, by the same token, when you hear someone over praised by a devoted or a loving friend, what about that? That's a compliment, and it's less dangerous to depend upon that, but certainly if you want the accurate facts, then you will study the remarks of a complimentary nature just as closely as you would study all others.

If I send somebody over to you for a job, I send along with them a very laudatory letter, get you on the telephone, give you a sales pitch about that person, and start telling you what a great person that person is. If you're an accurate thinker, you're going to know I'm rubbing it on really thick. You should be very careful of how much you should accept of what I'm saying about them.

You'd better do a little bit of outside investigating, isn't that right? I'm not trying to make a doubting Thomas out of you. I'm not trying to make a cynic out of you. I'm only trying to get your attention about the necessity to use this God-given brain to think accurately and search for the facts.

When you find the facts, they may not be what you were searching or looking for, but there are the facts. There are many people in the world who fool themselves. There's no worse fooling in the world than the fooling one does to him or herself.

Remember the old Chinese proverb that says, "Fool me once, shame on the man. Fool me twice, shame on me."

Then, these wishes often become fathers to facts. Many people have a bad habit of assuming facts to harmonize with their desires. Did you know that? So, you have to really look into the mirror when you're searching for the person who can do accurate thinking. You've got to put yourself under suspicion a little bit, too, don't you?

If you wish for a thing to be true, oftentimes you will assume it is true and will act as if it were true. If you love a person a great deal, you may overlook their faults, especially if you really and truly love them. So, really and truly we do need to watch ourselves in connection with those whom we admire most, until they have proven themselves entirely.

I have admired many people who turned out to be very dangerous. I think most my troubles have come from trusting other people too much. Why did I trust them?

I trusted them, because they seemed like really nice people. Be careful of the people that seem really nice.

Don't be too hard on the man who steps on your corns and causes you to reexamine yourself. That man may be the most important friend you have ever had in your entire lifetime. That person may irritate you or cause you to examine yourself very carefully. We all like to meet and associate with people who agree with us. That's just human nature.

Oftentimes, these people who you associate with and who agree with you can come to the point to where they take advantage of you and do take advantage of you. Information is abundant and most of it free. Facts have an elusive habit, and generally there is a price attached to them. The price is painstaking labor in examining them for their accuracy.

This question of how you know is the favorite question of the thinker. When a thinker hears a statement they can't accept, they immediately say to the speaker, "How do you know? What is your source of information?"

This is the business of asking people to identify their source of knowledge. Oftentimes, if you have the slightest doubt, you'll put the person right out on a limb, and they won't be able to tell you how they know. If you ask them how they know, they will say, "I believe so."

What right should anyone have to believe anything unless it's based upon something? You can give some background for it. I believe there's a God. There are many people who say they believe there's a God who couldn't give you the slightest evidence of Him if you backed them into a corner.

I can give you evidence.

When I say that I believe there's a God, then you ask me how do I know. I don't have so much evidence with anything else in the entire world as I do with the existence of a Creator. The orderliness of this universe could not go on and on eons and eons of times ad infinitum without a first cause or without a plan behind the universe. You know that's an absolutely true important fact. There are many people who try to prove the existence of God in various ways, but in my book of rules wouldn't be evidence at all.

Anything that exists, including God, is capable of proof.

Where there is no such proof available, it's safer to assume nothing exists. When no facts are available for the basis of an opinion, a judgment, or a plan, I want you to turn to logic for guidance. No one has ever seen God, but logic says He has to exist, or we couldn't be here without a first cause or a higher intelligence.

You need to be careful and pay high respect to those hunches, because that's infinite intelligence trying to break through the outer shell of your skull and let you use a little logic.

If you said your definite major purpose is to make a million dollars this coming year, what would be the first question you should ask yourself, do you think? How are you going to do it and what is your plan? Then what are you going to do about your plan? Are you going to accept your plan, or are you going to reject your plan?

You're going to weigh yourself, first of all, in your ability to get those million dollars. Then you would decide on what you're going to give in return for those million dollars. Then your logic would tell you whether your plan for doing it is probable, workable, and practical. That doesn't take an awful lot of intelligent thinking, but it's a vitally important thing you must do to make those million dollars.

You would go over your plan and analyze your plan.

You would analyze your capabilities.

You would analyze your past experiences.

You would analyze your past achievements.

You would analyze the people you're going to help make those million dollars. Then when you got through analyzing your plan, you would be able to tell whether or not you could do within this year what you said, or maybe it would take two years or three.

Accurate thinkers don't allow their emotions to run away with them. This leads up to a famous motto or epigram you may have seen quoted a lot of times in **Napoleon Hill's** books and lessons:

Whatever your mind can conceive and believe your mind can achieve.

Please don't misread that statement, by reading into it, whatever your mind can conceive and believe your mind will achieve. I said, "It can achieve." Do you get the line of difference between the two? It can achieve, but I don't know if it will achieve what you believe, because that's your belief, and that's completely up to you. Only you know that answer, the extent to which you use your own mind. The extent to which you intensify your own faith, the soundness of your own judgment, and your own plans will all be the self-determining factors entering into how well you carry out that famous motto or epigram.

Some acid tests now to be made to separate facts from information:

Scrutinize with unusual care everything you read in newspapers or hear over the radio. Form the habit of never accepting any statement as a fact merely because you read it or heard it expressed by someone. Statements bearing some proportion of fact often are intentionally and carelessly colored to give them an erroneous meaning.

A half-truth is more dangerous than an out-and out lie.

The half-truth part is more dangerous, because that half-truth part is liable to deceive somebody who understands half of it and thinks the whole of it is true.

Scrutinize everything you read in books, regardless of who wrote them. Never accept the works of any writer without asking the following questions and satisfying yourself as to the answers. These rules that I'm going to give you should apply to lectures, statements, speeches, or conversations.

- Is the writer, the speaker, the teacher, or the one making the statement a **recognized authority** on the subject on which he or she is speaking or writing?

That's the very first question you should ask.

- Does the writer or the speaker have any ulterior or self-interest motives other than imparting accurate information?

The motive that prompts an individual to write a book, make a speech in public, make a statement in public or in private conversation is a very important. If you can get at a man or woman's motive while their talking, you can tell pretty much how truthful they are by what they are saying.

Has a writer or the speaker a profit interest or some other interest on the subject he or she writes or speaks about? If you find out what a person's motive is, it would be impossible for them to fool you in the least, because you'd be able to smell them out.

- Is the writer or the speaker a person of sound judgment and not a fanatic on the subject, which he or she writes or speaks?

I have seen people go to the point of fanaticism. If you wanted to judge me, you wouldn't judge me on the kind of clothes I wear, how I cut my hair, how well I speak, or how poorly I write or speak. How would you judge me? You would judge me by how much influence I'm having for good or evil on other people. That's the way you would judge me. That's the way you would judge anybody else.

You might not like a man or woman's brand of religion or politics. If they're doing a great job in their field and helping a lot of people and doing no damage, never mind about their brand. Don't condemn them if they are doing more good than harm.

Before accepting as fact the statements made by a person, ascertain the motive which prompted that person to make the statement. Ascertain also the writer or speaker's reputation for truth and veracity. Scrutinize with unusual care all statements made by people who have a strong motive or objective they desire to attain through their statement.

Be equally as careful about accepting as fact the statements of overzealous people who have the habit of allowing his or her imagination run wild. Learn to be cautious and to use your own judgment no matter who is trying to influence you in the final analysis.

What do you do if you can't trust your own judgment?

Is there an answer in this book for that? There most certainly is an answer for that. There are a lot of times when an individual can't trust his or her own judgment because they don't know enough about the circumstances they are facing. He or she will have to turn to somebody with broader experience or a different education or a keener mind for analysis.

For instance, can you imagine a business succeeding made up of all master salesmen? Did you ever know of such a business? You'd think that wonderful master salesmen will go out and bring in all the business in the world? Sure, they will, and then spend all the money in the world bringing in the business.

You need a wet blanket person in every organization, and sometimes they are called "a hatchet man", a person who will cut through the red tape and everything else that gets in the way, and let the chips fall wherever they may. I wouldn't want to be a hatchet man, but I'd certainly want one in my organization if my operation were very extensive.

In seeking facts from others, do not disclose to them what facts you expect to find and why that statement was made.

If I called you on the phone and said, "By the way, you used to employ John Doe, and he's just applied to me for a job, and he seems like a wonderful man. What do you think?"

If he has any faults, I'll certainly not get them with that kind of a question, would I? If I really wanted to find out about John Doe who used to work for you, how would I go about getting the information? I wouldn't go about getting the information from you in the first place. I'd have a commercial credit company get an unbiased report on him from you.

You'd probably give out the facts to the credit rating company you wouldn't give out to me or to anybody else.

There's a lot of information you can get about a person if you know the right commercial credit agency through which to get the information.

If you go directly for information about a person, unless it's friendly and very favorable, then chances are you won't get the real facts. You'll get a varnished or watered-down set of facts, when you ask a person a question and give them the slightest idea as to what you expect the answer to be.

Then, most of the time you will get the answer you wanted.

Then, you'll be tickled to death with it, and you will fall flat with it later on.

Science is the art of organizing and classifying facts. That's what science means. To be sure you're dealing with facts, seek scientific sources for testing where possible. Men or women of science have neither the reason nor the inclination to modify or to change facts or to misrepresent them. They just don't have the reason; if they had that inclination, they would not be scientists. They'd be pseudo-scientists or fakes who assume to know things that they do not know.

There are some pseudo-scientists and fakes in the world who assume to know things that they really don't know.

Your emotions are not reliable, and before being influenced too far by your feelings, give your head a chance to pass judgment on the business at hand.

The head is more dependable than the heart, but what makes a good combination? Balancing, that's the idea, just balancing them so that both have an equal say. You'll pretty much come up with the right answer by doing that, and the person who forgets that generally regrets their neglect.

Here are the major enemies of sound thinking:

The great emotion of love stands right at the head of the list as an enemy of sound thinking. You might be asking yourself how in the world could the emotion of love interfere with anybody's thinking? If you were to say that, then I'd know right away you're still a young buck, and you haven't had very many love experiences.

If you've ever had any experience with love at all, then you know very well know how dangerous love is because it's like playing around with a grenade the pin removed.

When love starts exploding, it doesn't give any notice. Then hatred, anger, jealousy, fear, revenge, greed, vanity, egotism, the desire for something for nothing, and procrastination are all the major enemies of sound thinking.

You've got to be on the lookout for them constantly to be sure you're free of them, provided the thinking at hand is of importance to you, and maybe your whole destiny depends upon your thinking accurately. Isn't that a fact that it does?

Doesn't your destiny depend very largely on your accuracy or your lack of it in your own thinking? If that were not true, then what good would it be for the Creator to give you complete control over your own mind? What good would it be? The answer is that the mind is sufficient unto all your needs in life at least in this life span. I don't know about the preceding plane where you came from or the succeeding plane where you're going. I don't know about those planes. I do know a great deal about where I am today.

I have found how to influence my destiny here and can get a lot of pleasure. I can get a lot of joy, and I have made myself useful and justified myself having passed this way.

Why can I say that? I have discovered how to manipulate my own mind, to keep it under control, and to make it do the things I want it to do. I have learned to throw off the circumstances that I don't want, and if I don't find the circumstances I want, what do I do? I create them, because that's what a definite major purpose and the imagination are used for doing.

You should keep your mind an eternal question mark and question everything and everyone until you satisfy yourself you are dealing with facts. Do this quietly in the silence of your own mind and avoid being known as a doubting Thomas. Don't come out and question people orally. That's not going to get you anywhere, but question them silently. If you're too outspoken or too oral about your questioning, it puts people on notice, and then they cover up, and you don't get the accurate information.

Quietly go about seeking for accurate information, do some accurate thinking, and you will come up with the right answer. Be a good listener, but also be an accurate thinker as you listen. Which is the more profitable, to be a good speaker like Zig Ziglar, or to be a good analytical listener?

I don't know any other quality that would help an individual to get along better in the world than to be an effective enthusiastic speaker. I would follow that statement immediately by saying it's far more profitable for anybody to be a good listener, an analytical listener, than it is to be a good speaker. Let your mind be an eternal question mark.

You shouldn't become a cynic or a doubting Thomas. By that I mean no matter whom you're dealing with, deal with them on the basis of thinking accurately of every relationship you have. You'll get a lot more satisfaction out of that, and you'll also become more successful. If you're tactful as you go along and diplomatic, you'll have a lot more substantial friends than you would have by the old method of snap judgment.

Believe me, most of your friends will be friends worth having if you're an accurate thinker. Your thinking habits are the results of social heredity and physical heredity.

Through physical heredity you get everything you are physically, such as the stature of your body, the texture of your skin, and the color of your eyes and hair.

You're the total of all your ancestors back farther than you can ever remember or think. You have inherited a little of their good qualities and a little of their bad ones, and there's nothing you can do about that. It's static and fixed at birth.

By far the most important part of what you are today is the result of your social heredity and the environmental influences you have allowed to go into your mind, that you have accepted as part of your character.

Your conscience was given to you as a guide when all other sources of knowledge and facts have been exhausted in life.

Be careful to use it as a guide and not as a conspirator. Did you know the majority of people use their consciences as a conspirator instead of a guide? They so sell their conscience on the idea what they're doing is right, and then the conscience eventually falls in line and becomes a conspirator.

If you sincerely want to think accurately, there is a price you must pay for the ability which is not measurable in money. You must learn to examine carefully all your emotional feelings by submitting them to your sense of reason.

The point I'm making is be careful of what you set your heart on, because sometimes when you get it, you find out it's not what you wanted in the first place.

Have you ever seen people who paid too much for what they got? They wanted something so very badly, tried to get too much of it, and didn't get peace of mind and balancing of their lives along with what they set their heart upon.

These are people who became so obsessed with the importance of money, and what power and money would give to them. You must curb the habit of expressing an opinion not based upon facts or what you believe to be actual provable facts. You can do it, but it's dangerous for you, because then you have the responsibility of assuming what happens to you if you do express an opinion not based upon facts or what you believe to be actual acceptable provable facts.

You can fool yourself that way and go all the way through life fooling yourself by opinions that have no basis for existence.

You must master the habit of not being influenced by people in any manner whatsoever merely because you like them, or they are related to you, or they may have done you a favor. I know when you have gone the extra mile, you're going to put a lot of people under obligation to you. I want you to do that, because that's perfectly proper, and that's perfectly legitimate putting other people under obligation to you by helping them.

Nobody can find any fault with doing that for other people. But, be careful in being influenced by people just because they have done you a favor. I'm talking about the people for whom you've gone the extra mile.

You may be in a position where somebody has put you under obligation to an unwanted extent. You must form the habit of examining the motives of people who seek some benefit from or through your influence. You must control both your emotion of love and your emotion of hate in making decisions for any purpose, because either of these can unbalance your thinking habits. No person should ever make an important decision while they're angry.

In correcting children, for instance, it's a mistake to discipline children when you're angry, because nine times out of ten you'll do and say the wrong thing, and then do a lot more harm than good. That applies to a lot of grown-ups. If you're really angry, don't make decisions, and don't make statements to other people while you're mad, because they can come back on you and do you an awful lot of injury.

Self-discipline: You see, we have a chapter on self-discipline, remember? That plays right along with this chapter, doesn't it? There are lots of times, if you're going to be an accurate thinker, you've got to have a lot of self-discipline. You have got to refrain from saying and doing a lot of things you'd like to say and do. Bide your time for what you say and do. There's always a time for you to say and do everything.

Time what you say and do properly, and accurate

thinkers do that. They don't just fly off the handle and start their mouths to going and go off and leave them. Accurate thinkers carefully study the effect on the listener of every word they utter even before it's uttered. Don't make any decisions or plans until you have carefully weighed what the effect may be on you and on other people.

I can think of a lot of things I could do that would benefit me that wouldn't benefit you or anybody else. I wouldn't engage in any of them, because eventually I'd have to pay the price.

Whatever you do to or for another person you do to or for yourself, and it comes back to you greatly multiplied.

That's another thing that comes under the heading of accurate thinking. You learn not to do anything that you don't want to come back and affect you and you will have to give account to later on.

You must recognize before accepting as facts the statements of other people. It may be beneficial if you ask them how they came by the so-called facts. When someone expresses an opinion ask how they know their opinion is sound.

I don't want an opinion. I want the facts, and then I'll put them together in my own way, says the accurate thinker. You must learn to examine with extraordinary care all statements of a derogatory nature made by one person against another, because the very nature of such a statement brands them not being without bias, and that's putting it very politely.

You must overcome the habit of trying to justify a decision you have made, which has turned out to be unsound. Accurate thinkers just don't do that; they reverse themselves just as quickly as they make the decision if they find they're wrong. If you are an accurate thinker, you will never use the term "they say" or "I heard."

Accurate thinkers in repeating things they have heard first identify the source and attempt to establish its dependability. You know it's not very easy to become an accurate thinker. Have you reached that conclusion already? There's quite a little bit you have to pay in order to have it, but it's worth trying. If you're not an accurate thinker people are going to take advantage of you throughout life. You're not going to get as much out of life like you'd like to. You're not going to be well satisfied and a well-balanced person without accurate thinking.

In order to think accurately you've got to have a set of rules to go by. You'll find if you study this chapter carefully, you'll start doing some thinking of your own, and start putting into practice some of these principles of separating facts from information. Start separating the facts themselves into two classes: important and unimportant.

If you just make simple steps alone, this chapter will have very much more than have justified itself, and this chapter alone could well be worth a thousand times as much as you paid for the entire book. If it teaches you just to do those simple things, start separating facts from information. Be sure that you're dealing with facts, and then take the facts after dealing with them and break them down and throw off all the unimportant facts you have been wasting so much time with.

12

LEARNING FROM ADVERSITY AND DEFEAT

There is one thing in the world individuals do not like to undergo, its adversity, unpleasant circumstances, and defeat.

If I have evaluated circumstances properly and taken inventory of the laws of nature properly, it was intended that we all must undergo adversities, defeat, failure, and opposition. It was out of the adversities and opposition that I met with that I grew the strength, wisdom, and the ability to complete this book.

If I were to go back over my past, and I had my choice, I would have no doubt made life a whole lot easier. We are all inclined to do that in life, find the line of least resistance. Did you know taking the line of least resistance makes all rivers and some men crooked? It's a very common habit for us to do that, because we don't want to pay the price of intense effort no matter what we're doing.

The mind is just like any part of the physical body. It atrophies, withers away, and becomes weak through disuse. When you meet with any problems, circumstances, or instances that force you to do any thinking, that is one of the finest things that can happen to any individual, because without a motive, you're probably not going to do very much thinking.

There are forty major reasons or causes of failure.

There are more than twice as many causes of failure as there are principles of success.

There are seventeen principles of success, and some of them combined are responsible for all successful achievements.

There are more than forty major causes of failure.

These are not all of them. These are just the major causes of failure.

Self-examination is one of the most profitable things anyone can indulge in. Sometimes we don't like to do it or really to want to do it, but it's a very necessary thing for us to know ourselves as we are, and especially our weaknesses.

In putting out a practical philosophy of success, it is necessary for me to tell you what you should do to succeed and the things not to do to fail. You can grade yourself from zero to a hundred, meaning if you're 100 percent free, grade yourself 100 percent. If you're only 50 percent free, grade yourself 50 percent. When you get through, add the total up and divide it by the forty causes of failure, and you will get your general average rating on the control of the things that cause men and women to fail.

1. **The habit of drifting with circumstances without definite aims or plans**

    If you don't fall into the habit of drifting and you make decisions quickly and lay out plans and you follow those plans and know exactly where you're going, you're on the way, you can grade yourself 100 percent.

2. **Unfavorable physical hereditary foundation at birth**

    This could be a cause of failure or a cause of success.

    Some of the most successful people in the world have been handicapped by bad afflictions at birth.

3. **"Meddlesome curiosity" in connection with other people's business and affairs**

    Curiosity is a great thing because if you weren't curious you'd never learn anything, or you'd never investigate. Notice the wording here, "meddlesome curiosity" with other people's affairs, meaning something that doesn't really concern you.

    As you grade yourself, go back into your past experiences and determine to what extent you have control of these weaknesses.

4. **Lack of a definite major purpose as a lifetime goal**

I've been talking about having one for a long time throughout the entire book.

Now you're putting down the lack of a definite major purpose.

5. Inadequate schooling

The most outstanding things I have learned from life is there very little relationship between schooling and success. Some of the most successful people in the world have been people with the least amount of formal education.

I really want you to think this one over very carefully.

A lot of people go through life as failures, and they alibi themselves out of it and kid themselves into believing they are failures, because they don't have a college education.

If you came out of college with the feeling you should be paid for what you know instead of what you do with what you know. Then obviously that college education hasn't done you very much good until you meet old man destiny.

He's just standing around the corner with a stuffed   club, and it's not stuffed with cotton. You will find out you're not going to be paid for what you know. You're going to be paid for what you do with what you know, or what you get other people to do for you.

6. **Lack of self-discipline**

   This means excess in eating, drinking, and indifference to opportunities for self-advancement and improvement.

7. **Lack of ambition to aim above mediocrity**

   Here's a humdinger of all humdingers. How much ambition do you have and where are you going in your life? What do you want to get out of life, and what are you going to settle for in life?

   I had a soldier friend of mine in the Army who just wanted to settle for an MRE and a place to sleep every night. I wouldn't let him do it, and I talked him into settling for a much higher rate. He would become a squad leader the following year.

   I hope I have as much success with you as Mr. Hill did with me in stepping up your ambition to where you're not willing to settle for a penny. Aim high. You may not get as far as you aim, but you will certainly get further than if you didn't aim at all. Get your sights raised up, be ambitious, and be determined you're going to become in the future what you have failed to become in the past.

8. **Ill health often due to wrong thinking and improper diet**

I don't know to what extent you've been coddling yourself or babying yourself with this and that and the other imaginary ailments.

9. Unfavorable environmental influences during childhood

You will find out the influences of a child growing up in poverty are such of a negative nature they go all the way through life being negative.

I'm quite convinced if I would have been positive and followed my dream to become a rich and famous racecar driver, I would have truly become a great race car driver.

10. Lack of persistence in following through with one's duties

What's the main reason people do not follow through, do the thing right, and see it's done right? Lack of a motive. They don't want to do it badly enough, and these people find a lot of alibis from following through.

Do you think it's profitable for you to get into the habit of following through when you undertake something, or is it profitable for you to permit yourself to be sidetracked?

If I had been afraid of criticism, I couldn't have gotten anywhere in my life. I could have never completed this book. I finally got to the point eventually at which I really courted criticism, because that only put the fight in me. I found out when that fight was in me, I did a much better job and carried through way much better.

There are some people who fail because they lack that driving force that causes them to carry through, especially when the going is hard.

No matter what you're doing, you're going to run into a period when the going is hard. If it's a new business, you'll probably need finances you don't have in the beginning. If it's a profession, you will need clients you don't have in the beginning.

If it's a new job, you will need recognition with your employer you don't have in the beginning. The going is always hard with people in the beginning, and that's where you will need to follow through.

11. A negative mental attitude

When you see a donut, do you see the hole first or the donut? When you eat the donut, you don't eat the hole; you eat the donut.

There are some people in the world that when they come across a problem, they are like the person who sees the hole in the donut and growls about it, because somebody took so much out of the nice cake.

What is the result of a person who has the habit of

allowing their mind to become and remain negative? A negative mind repels, and a positive mind attracts people who harmonize with your mental attitude and your character. Remember that old saying, "Birds of a feather flock together "? The negative birds flock to the negative mind, and the positive birds flock to the positive mind.

Who has control over your mind, or who determines whether it is positive or negative? There's where you should grade yourself to the extent that you exercise your prerogative. That's the most precious thing you have on the face of this earth or ever will have. The only thing you have complete and unchallenged and unchallengeable right of control over is the right to make your mind positive, and then to keep it that way, or allow the circumstances to make it negative. You really must work at it if you're going to keep your mind positive all the time.

For what reason? So many negative people around you in the world and so many circumstances that are negative, you must guard against becoming part of those negative influences, unless you create positive ones in your mind.

Do you have a very clear concept of the difference between a negative mind and a positive mind? Can you picture what happens in the chemistry of the brain when you're more positive than negative? Have you ever demonstrated or experienced in your own life the differences between your achievements when you are afraid and the achievements when you are not afraid?

When I started doing my research for this book, it was right after the 9-1-1 attacks when the country was in chaos. I was doing my research in a negative mental attitude and writing in a negative mental attitude. I wasn't very pleased with what just happened. I was also rushing while writing to get this philosophy spread all over the world to help stop the violence in the world. A reader will pick up exactly the mental attitude a writer is in when he or she writes a book, no matter what kind of language or terminology they use.

I sat down in front of my computer when I was in a new frame of mind, on the beam, 100 percent positive, and took my time writing this book in a positive frame of mind, and that is what has made this book click.

If you want to get people to cooperate with you, if you want to sell people something, or if you want to make a good impression upon people, don't come near them until you're in a positive frame of mind.

The reason I have emphasized this point so much is I want to give you a chance to grade yourself accurately on that one.

You'll want to grade yourself on the average state of mind you maintain every day, and not just on the state of mind you maintain for a short time.

I'll give you a good rule to go by which will allow you to determine to a large extent whether you're more positive than negative during the day. Observe how you feel when you wake up and start to get up out of bed. If you're not in a good frame of mind, it's because of a lot of thought habits that have preceded that hour or the day before that have been negative.

You can make yourself very ill by allowing your mind to become negative, and it will reflect itself in the next morning particularly.

When you come out of sleep, you're fresh from coming from under the influence of your subconscious mind. Your conscious mind has been off duty, goes back on duty, and finds a mess to clean up which the subconscious mind has been stirring up all night long. If you wake up full of joy, and you want to get out to do what you want to do for the day, chances are you have been pretty positive the day before and maybe several days before.

12. Lack of control over the emotions both the negative and the positive ones

Did you know it's just as important to control your positive emotions as it is your negative ones? Why should you want to control the emotion of love, for instance? The emotion of love can get you into hot water and can scald you.

What about the desire for financial gain? There could be such a thing as working that emotion up to where you want to get too much and get it the wrong way. I'm eternally grateful I swapped my youth for wisdom and learned a better way of earning finances for myself in the right way and without having it given to me.

13. The desire for something for nothing

Are you ever troubled with the desire for something for nothing, the desire for something for less than its value, or the desire for something without being willing to give adequate compensation for it? Who of us hasn't felt that way at one time or another?

What you can do is start finding your faults and start getting rid of them.

I'm giving you a chance to come face-to-face with yourself, and be a trial judge, defendant, and prosecutor all at one time. Then you can make the decision finally, and if you make it accurately. It would be far better for you to find your faults, because then you're not going to spin any alibis to get rid of them.

14. Lack of the habit of reaching decisions promptly and firmly

Do you reach decisions promptly and firmly or do you reach decisions very slowly and allow the first person that comes along reverse you on a decision? Do you allow the circumstances of life to reverse your decision without a sound reason?

To what extent do you stand by your decision after you made them? Under what circumstance would you reverse a decision you made incidentally?

You should never make a decision and say, "That's it, I'm going to stand by it forever." Something might develop later on that would prompt you to reverse that decision.

There are some people who are known as stubborn, and when once they make a decision right or wrong, they'd die by it. I've seen people who would just rather die than reverse himself or herself or have somebody else reverse them on a decision. Of course, you're not like that if you're really indoctrinated with this philosophy. You may have been like that once, but you're not going to be like that now after reading this book.

15. One or more of the seven basic fears

I'll not dwell on this one. It's a wonderful world we are living in and a wonderful life. I'm glad I'm here and doing just what I'm doing. If unpleasant circumstances cross my path, I'm very glad for that, because I'll find out if I'm stronger than the circumstance. As long as I can conquer circumstances and go over them, I'm not going to worry about any unpleasant circumstances. I'm not going to worry about the people who oppose me, or the people who don't like me, or the people who say mean things about me. What I would worry about is if people said mean things about me, and I examined myself and found out they are telling the truth. As long as they're not telling the truth, I can stand back and laugh at how foolish they are and how much damage they are doing to themselves.

16. The wrong selection of a mate in marriage

Don't grade yourself too quickly on this one and make a snap judgment. If you have made a 100 percent mistake on that, maybe you can do something about correcting it, like maybe re-selling yourself. I've known of that being done, haven't you?

There are some people who believe all marriages are made in heaven. It would be a great thing if they were made in heaven. I've seen some not made in heaven. I'm not sure where they might have been made. They were certainly not made in heaven.

I've seen some business marriages or relationships that were not made in heaven. These business associates not working together in a spirit of perfect harmony. There's no business on the face of this earth that can succeed unless the people at the top level are working in harmony. There is no household that can be a joy or a place you want to go to more than you want to come away from unless there's harmony.

That harmony starts with loyalty then dependability and then the ability to do the job.

That's the way I would evaluate people.

If I wanted to select a person for a high position.

The first thing I would look for is if the person was loyal to the people to whom they owed loyalty.

The next thing I would look for would be dependability, that I can depend on them to be at the right place at the right time and do the right thing.

The last thing would be the ability to do the job.

17. **Over caution in business and professional relationships**

Have you seen people who wouldn't trust their own mother-in-law? I knew a man so cautious he had a special hiding place inside his closet in a pair of his boots, and he would hide his money from his wife. Wasn't he a honey? I'm sure his wife loved him.

18. **Lack of all forms of caution in all human relationships**

Have you seen people start their mouths going, go off, leave, and never mind what they're going to say or what effect their words will have on other people? You've seen people like that, haven't you?

No caution whatsoever. No discrimination, no diplomacy, and no consideration of what they're going to do to other people with their words. I've seen people with tongues sharper than a double-edge Gillette blade that has never been used. They would start cutting and walk away from you.

I've seen people who would sign anything a salesman put in front of them without even reading it. They wouldn't even read the big type, let alone the little type. Have you seen people like that? Of course, you're not like that, are you? You can be over cautious, and you can be under cautious. Where would you find the happy medium?

You would find the happy medium in the chapter on accurate thinking where you examine carefully the things you're going to do before you do them, not afterward. You will evaluate your words before you express them and not afterward. You know it's going to be a little bit difficult for you to grade yourself accurately on that one. To be perfectly candid with you, it would be a little bit difficult for me to grade myself accurately on number 17 and this one. There have been a lot of times in my life when I wasn't very cautious at all. I think most of my troubles have come from trusting too many people.

Mr. Hill had that same problem with people. These people would go around the country and flimflam his name, not using it wisely. I wouldn't want to become so cautious I didn't trust anybody for anything. You'd get no joy out of living if you had to live like that all the time.

19. Wrong choice of associates in one's occupation or calling

Have you ever heard of people getting into trouble because they were associated with the wrong kind of people? I have never seen a youngster go bad, go wrong, or get into bad habits except by being influenced, or listening to some other person.

20. Wrong selection of a vocation or total neglect to make a choice of a vocation

Ninety-eight out of every hundred people would grade zero on this one. Since now that you have had a chance to become indoctrinated with chapter 1 on a definite major purpose, you can grade yourself much higher. This one you can either grade zero or one hundred percent. There is no halfway point. You can't grade fifty or sixty or any other amount on this one. You either have one, or you don't have one.

21. Lack of concentration or effort

You split and divide your interest among a lot of different things. One person is not strong enough. Life is too short, unless you do learn the art of concentrating everything you've got on one thing at a time, then following through on that one thing and do a great job.

22. Lack of budget control over income and expenditures

How does the average person manage the question of a budget? It's usually controlled by the amount of credit they can get from other people when the credit shuts down on them, the more or less slack-off. But, until that happens, they run wild with spending.

A good business firm would go bankrupt if it didn't have a system of control over its income and expenditures. That's what a controller in an organization is used for. They call them a "wet blanket". Every successful business of any size needs a wet blanket, a person who controls the assets of the company and keeps them from getting away at the wrong time and the wrong way.

23. The failure to budget and use time to the best advantage

Time is the most precious thing we have. We have twenty-four hours every day. Eight hours we must devote to sleep if we're going to have good health. We have another eight hours to make a living. Then, here in America as free citizens we can do anything in the world we want to do with those remaining eight hours. We can sin. We can spend. We can establish good habits. We can establish bad habits. We reeducate ourselves and our minds during those eight hours. But, the question remains what actually are you doing with those eight hours?

There is going to be a determining factor as to how well you grade yourself on that particular question:

Do you have a system of actually making all of your time count? Of course, you have the first sixteen hours practically taken care of automatically. Those remaining eight hours are something you can do pretty much anything with. It's flexible.

24. Lack of controlled enthusiasm

Enthusiasm is among the most valuable of the emotions beyond a question of a doubt. That's provided you can turn it on and turn it off just like you would water at the spigot or like the switch of an electric light.

If you can turn on your enthusiasm when you want to turn it on, then turn it off whenever you want to turn it off, you can grade yourself 100 percent. If you lack the ability to do that, you will grade yourself zero.

How does a person go about controlling their enthusiasm? Have you ever thought about your willpower? You have the power of will, and its purpose is for discipline over your mind.

You can make your mind whatever you want it to be. You can form whatever kind of habits you want.

Which is the worst, no enthusiasm, a cold fish, or red-hot enthusiasm out of control? I'd say both are bad.

There was a time when I could turn on my anger much more quickly than I could turn on my enthusiasm. That's something you'll have to overcome, the ability to turn on any of your emotions or to turn them off.

25. Intolerance

This means a closed mind based on ignorance or prejudice in connection with religious, racial, political, or economic ideas. If you could say you have an open mind on all subjects toward all people at all times, then you might not be a human but a saint.

There are times I suppose if you made up your mind to be open minded on all these things, you could for a little while. Suppose you can't be open-minded toward all people at all times on all subjects? What's the next best thing to do? Be tolerant some of the time. The more you try that sometime, it will take more and more time. Then eventually you will get to where tolerance will become a habit with you instead of intolerance.

There are some individuals in the world, regretfully, when these individuals meet other people they immediately begin to look for all the bad things they don't like in the other people.

This individual always seems to find all the bad things they don't like in other people.

Then I notice this other type person is always much more successful, happy, and welcoming when they meet a person, whether it's an acquaintance or a stranger. This other type person immediately begins to look for not only the good qualities in the other person, also compliments them, says something, or does something to show they recognize the good qualities instead of the bad.

I get a great feeling when somebody walks up to me and says, "I want to tell you, Mr. West, how much good I got out of your book. I got my first definite major purpose."

I really thrive on that. I really love it, unless, of course, they lay it on too thick.

Even pussycats, as bad natured as they are, if you stroke them on the back, they will curl up their tails and begin to purr. Cats are not very friendly, but you can make them friendly if you do the things cats like.

26. **Failure to cooperate with others in the spirit of harmony**

I suppose there could be circumstances where your failure to cooperate with others would be justified, or are there? I could say there are circumstances where you would fail to cooperate. I come into contact with people who want me to do things for them I can't possibly do.

If someone wants my influence, if someone wants me to write letters of recommendation, or if someone wants me to make telephone calls for them, I can't cooperate with them unless I'm sold on what or whom I'm cooperating with. You would be like that, too.

27. **Possession of power or wealth not based on merit or earned**

On this one you should have no trouble grading yourself accurately.

28. **Lack of the spirit of loyalty to those to whom loyalty is due.**

If you have loyalty in your heart to those whom loyalty is due, you can grade yourself 100 percent. But, unless you practice that all the time, you wouldn't grade yourself 100 percent. You would grade yourself something lower on that one. On any of these causes of failure if you grade yourself lower than 50 percent, you should put a cross mark by it, and go back for the study of that particular cause of failure.

You should have all these causes of failure at least 50 percent under control.

29. The habit of forming opinions not based upon known facts

It would be great if you can give yourself a good rating on this one. If you grade below 50 percent, you should begin to start working yourself up right away, and stop having opinions, unless, of course, you base them on facts, or what you believe to be actual provable facts.

There are some people in the world who have opinions about everything. They could run the country better than the president. They can work their friends over and improve them.

If you examine most of them very carefully, these people are not doing too well themselves.

30. Egotism and vanity not under control

Egotism is a great thing, and vanity is a great thing. If you didn't have a little vanity, you wouldn't wash your neck or face, or have your hair permed or whatever it is the women do to their hair. You need to have a little vanity and a little pride. You can have too much, can't you?

I think lipstick is a wonderful thing if it doesn't stain my clothes. You can have too much lipstick and rouge on the face, can't you? I think nature is a pretty good old hand at painting faces just right. When I see an older woman painting her face up to look sixteen again, she's not fooling me.

The human ego is great as long as you have it under control. I've never seen a successful person yet who didn't have great confidence in their ability to do anything they started out to do. One of the purposes of this philosophy you're reading is to enable you to build up your ego to where it will do for you anything you want it to do, no matter what it is in your life.

There are some people whose ego needs to be trimmed down a little bit. But, I'd say there are very many more people who need a buildup than the ones who need a squishing. Many people need a buildup of their ego, because they have allowed the circumstances of life to whip them down. These great people have been whipped down until they've got no fight left in them, no courage and no applied faith.

31. Lack of vision and imagination

I have never been able to determine if this great capacity for vision and imagination is an inherited or an acquired quality. I'm pretty sure in my case it was inherited. I had a lot of imagination back to the earliest days that I can remember.

32. Unwillingness to go the extra mile

If you have the habit of going the extra mile, and you've learned to get great joy out of going the extra mile, chances are you're going to put a lot of people under obligation to you. They don't mind being under obligation to you on that basis.

If you have enough people obligated to you, there's no reason why you can't make legitimate use of those people, through their influence, their education, and their ability to help you succeed in whatever you're doing.

Do you know how to get anybody to do whatever you want him or her to do? Do something for them first. That's as good a definition I could use if I thought about it for 50 years. Look how easy it is to do something nice for another person. You don't even have to ask them. If you do want to have a great long list of people standing ready as an army to help you, do something nice for them.

What are you doing to cultivate that army in advance of the time of need? You will have to build up something called "goodwill" in advance. Then the timing has to be right.

There are some people who will go the extra mile only for the sake of expediency. They do it just to put you under obligation. They don't time it sufficiently to allow you to forget about it. Then, they turn right around after doing you a favor and ask you for two or three more favors.

If I had to select one principle with which you can do the most for people, I'd say it's the principle of going the extra mile. That's one thing anybody can control that wants to control. You don't have to ask anybody for the privilege of going out of your way to be nice and to be of help to other people. The very moment you start doing it, you profit by the law of contrast, because the majority of people around you are not doing it.

33. Desire for revenge of a real or imaginary grievance

Which is the worst? A desire for a revenge for an injury somebody has done to you, or the desire for revenge for an imaginary grievance? What happens to you when you have a desire for revenge or grievances for any reason whatsoever? Does it hurt the other person? It hurts you, makes you negative, and even poisons your mind. Any kind of negative mental attitude will get into your blood and interfere with your sound health.

34. The habit of producing alibis instead of satisfactory results

To what extent do you immediately begin to look for an alibi when you make a mistake?

What about when something you did doesn't turn out just quite right? Do you neglect to do the thing you should have done? Do you face the music? Do you conjure up a set of alibis to justify what you did, or what you have neglected to do?

I'll say if you're an average person, the chances are in the majority of the cases you'll look for an alibi to justify what you do or what you refrain from doing. I'm sure you will not be an average person now after reading this book. That's a weakness and a crutch you're leaning on.

You will face the music and acknowledge your mistakes and acknowledge your weaknesses. You will acknowledge your errors. Self-confession is a great thing. It does something for the soul when you really know what your faults are and confess them honestly. You don't have to spread them to the whole world.

35. Lack of dependability

This one perhaps will be a little bit hard for you to grade yourself on, but generally speaking, you know whether you're a dependable person or not. You know if your performance in your occupation or your job is dependable.

You know if your relationship with your family and your children is that of a dependable family man or family woman. You know if you're dependable with people in your credit relations when you buy things on credit.

Isn't it a great thing to have dependability among your loved ones, knowing they're not going to let you down on any score at any time for any reason?

If you have two people like that in your entire lifetime that are dependable under all circumstances, you are really a very fortunate person.

36. Unwillingness to assume responsibilities commensurate with one's desire for compensation

You desire the good things, the good income, the nice home, the nice car, the nice income. Are you willing to assume the necessary responsibilities that entitle you to all those things? What's the point you're grading yourself on?

37. The failure to obey your conscience when it seems advantageous not to do so

Are there times when you tell your conscience to just step aside for a few moments, and say, "Don't look right now, because there's a little transaction of business I want to attend to that's a little bit off color."

I'm not going to ask you to vote on this one. I wouldn't want to do that to you. I think you might get away with that a few times. I think if you got into the habit of doing that, it would convert your conscience into a conspirator and endure all the mean things you ever might want to do.

That would be bad.

That conscience was given to you by an all-wise Creator. If you're on good terms with your conscience and really respond to that conscience under every circumstance and let it be your guide, you are a very fortunate person. You have been using that conscience properly. If you are undecided and you make that conscience step aside, you might need to grade yourself low and begin to build yourself up on that score.

I think it's a great thing that God set up in every individual a judge advocate, so to speak, to sit over all their thoughts, and tell them when they are right and wrong.

38. The habit of unnecessarily worrying over the things you cannot control

If you can't get control over the things you're worrying about, what can you do? You can adjust yourself in a positive mental attitude, so it will not let you get down on yourself.

You can transfer the worry over onto another subject where you can control the thing you're worrying about.

39. Neglect to recognize the difference between failure and temporary defeat

What is failure anyhow? When you accept it as such, no matter what the conditions are. Is failure ever failure until you accept it as such? No; it's temporary defeat perhaps, but certainly not failure.

If you took no for an answer every time you are a salesman, you'd never make a living. It's much easier for people to say no than yes when they don't mean it at all. They just mean they haven't yet been broken down by a good salesman.

40. Lack of flexibility in adjusting to the varying circumstances

It may be necessary at times for you to go along with unsavory bedfellows, these people you don't like. You can go along with them until they drop out of your life. You can have it out with them right where you stand. If you did that, you'd probably get the worse of it. You can wear them out, walk them to death, and go along with them for a time.

If you make an incident out of everything you dislike in people, you will always be in difficulty through life. If you let these things that are food for incidents pass by, did you know time is a wonderful cure, a wonderful agent, and the greatest doctor of everything on the face of this earth? (Is it called Mother Time or Father Time?)

There is not a day that goes by in your life you couldn't make an incident out of something or have an unpleasant scene with somebody if you would allow yourself to do it.

You need to cultivate being flexible and adjust yourself to the circumstances you don't like without going down with any of them. You may have a very peculiar cause of failure I haven't mentioned.

I have given you a pretty good catalog of the things that cause people to fail. You can eliminate every one of those causes of failure, and you can almost do it instantaneously. That is one of the most interesting things about this list of the forty things that cause people to fail. They represent things you can do something about today.

What would be the use of having you make this analysis if you couldn't do anything about them? Again, you can eliminate every one of these causes of failure, and you can do it almost instantaneously. There are a few of these that will take a little time for you to develop into a more positive habit. But, for the most part, every one of these causes a failure you could wipe out of your character this very day by becoming self-determined to develop a more agreeable set of circumstances.

No matter what your adversity may have been in your past, go back after you read this chapter for the last ten years.

Then begin to search where the seed of an equivalent benefit was, even though you didn't find it the first time and haven't used it yet.

It's very difficult to find the seed of an equivalent benefit in an unpleasant circumstance while the wound is still open and hurting. There again, timing is important. If you'll give it a little time and make up your mind, you're not going to go down under the circumstance. You will find you will have learned something of benefit from it.

Until you have learned to be tolerant with those who do not always agree with you, until you have cultivated the habit of saying some kind word to those whom you do not admire, until you have formed the habit of looking for the good instead of the bad there is in others, you will be neither successful nor happy.

13

COOPERATION

There are two kinds of cooperation: one is based upon force or coercion, and the other is voluntary action based on motive. The majority of all circumstances of cooperation are based upon some form of force or coercion.

Employees oftentimes cooperate with their employers, but there's a certain amount of coercion and a certain amount of fear that if they don't cooperate, they will lose their jobs.

There are other circumstances where the employees cooperate with the employer, because the employer has made it so beneficial to work at that place they do it willingly.

Any kind of coercion or any type of force is not desirable, because individuals only cooperate on that basis as long as they have to. Then when it gets to the point where they don't have to any longer, they kick over the traces.

Relatively speaking, there is a small percentage of employers throughout the United States who understand the advantage of having their employees co-operate with them on a willing basis of friendliness based upon the benefits they extend to those employees.

Cooperation differs from the mastermind principle in that it's based upon coordination of effort without necessarily involving the principle of a definite major purpose or the principle of a spirit of perfect harmony.

An army of men in the military service working under their superior officers represent a tremendous amount of power based upon cooperation. It does not necessarily mean those men like to be there, or they like what they are doing.

Cooperation based on the mastermind principle is the medium by which "Great Personal Power" may be attained, and no one has ever acquired such power without the aid of these principles, an important fact that places them in a category of the indispensable.

Cooperation is indispensable in four major relationships: in the home, in one's job or profession, in social relationships, and in support of our form of government and free enterprise. Certainly, these are a must, and if every citizen cooperated in those four respects, we would have a much better country than we have today.

Here are some examples of cooperation not based on the mastermind principle: soldiers working under military regulations, employees working under rules of employment, and government officials working under the laws of the nation, professional men like lawyers, doctors, and dentists who work under rules of their ethics of their profession, and citizens of a nation existing under a dictator.

Observe the manner in which cooperative effort assumes greater powers when the principle of cooperation is combined with the mastermind principle. When the government officials were working in a spirit of perfect harmony and supported by a majority of the people as in the case of Roosevelt's first term in office, and when the emergency of an "economic depression" supplied motives for harmony with that motive being a desire for "economic recovery" affecting all of the people, there was never a finer illustration of power attained through the combination of the principle of cooperation and the American mastermind principle.

There was a great emergency going on, and they had to close ranks and get behind him whether they agreed with his political principles or not. They did that on a grand scale for a time, but as soon as the emergency passed or was softened, that combination of the American mastermind principle and cooperation began to disintegrate. Before Roosevelt got out of office, there was enough upheaval, lack of harmony, and a lot of other things that caused many people worry and annoyance, not to mention loss.

John West

While Mr. Hill was publishing the Golden Rule magazine, he got a hurry-up call from Mr. Nash of the Nash Clothing Company to come over to Cincinnati to see him. When Mr. Hill got there, he found that Mr. Nash was in trouble: he was really bankrupt. For no reason that Mr. Nash could explain, a business that had been profitable for years was suddenly unprofitable. The business dropped off to where they didn't even have enough to make their payroll.

When Mr. Hill went over the situation with Mr. Nash, he said there is only one thing that could be done to save the business. If they could work out a plan whereby all the employees would take a new lease in life and put their heart and soul into the business, they could save the business.

They all had worked out a plan whereby they would receive at the end of the year, in addition to their regular salaries, a bonus consisting of a percentage of the profits. Mr. Nash called all his employees together, got up, and told them what he had in mind.

Mr. Nash said, "I think I should tell you, first of all, that the company is bankrupt. We don't have enough money to make this coming week's payroll. For a long time, the business has been going downhill. I have noticed that all the employees are losing interest, and the enthusiasm that used to prevail is no longer here. Unless, we can recapture that spirit of enthusiasm and everyone jump in and do something, why, we're all going to end up in the same boat, namely bankrupt.

I have a plan, and I think it will work. It's based upon the Golden Rule. If we all come down Monday morning, and start in on a new basis with the same mental attitude that we had ten years ago when we were all thriving, I'll pay you as soon as we can make the wages, including the back wages that I'll not be able to pay you this coming week. If we make a go of it, at the end of the year we'll divide the profits on the same basis that will give you the same standing as a stockholder in the company."

Mr. Hill and Mr. Nash went to lunch and had been gone about an hour when this messenger came over and called them away from their lunch. The employees got together and decided not only were they going to accept Mr. Nash's proposition, they all came down the next day with their savings in old socks and tin cans and laid $16,000 in cash on Mr. Nash's desk.

The employees said, "There it is, Mr. Nash. If that's the way you feel about us, then this is the way we feel about you. We earned this money down here, and it isn't much, and if it'll do you any good, then use it. When you can pay it back, you can pay it back, and if you can't pay it back, that's all right, too."

You see, they had caught the real spirit of cooperation.

The company began to thrive, and before Mr. Nash died some ten years later, it became the most prosperous mail order clothing business in the whole United States. This was the exact same business at the exact same location making the same kind of clothes with the same people doing the work, failing one day and starting to succeed on a grand scale the very next day.

There was a change in what? There was a change of mental attitude, and what caused them to change their mental attitude was the fear of losing their jobs. They had a motive.

Mr. Nash inspired them with his sincerity and purpose in making them that kind of an offer. They were touched by that kind of offer, and when you get any group of individuals working together on that basis, they will all work together, will meet those problems, and meet them successfully.

Then, for the rotary clubs and their members throughout the world, there's a great illustration of the mastermind principle and harmony in the ranks. Napoleon Hill was a member of the first group, whose original purpose was to honor Paul Harris and to help build up his legal practice without violating his ethics. The rotary club finally grew bigger than that purpose, and the purpose became the idea of developing fellowship among the members.

You don't do anything in this world without a motive, and there must be a motive to inspire everything you do or everything you refrain from doing. The only person that does things without a motive is an insane person, because he or she doesn't have to have a motive.

The opportunity to get a higher compensation and promotion is one of the most outstanding motives for gaining friendly cooperation. Wherever that has been put into use in any business that I know about, there has always been a very beneficial and very profitable return. Recognition for personal initiative, a pleasing personality, and outstanding work is a strong motive to inspire cooperation by giving the person recognition when you know they have done a great job. Then do something about it when an employee does a great job.

I know some employers who have a record of the birth dates of all the male employees and their families, and every birthday, they all get presents from him with a card signed by him in person.

These kinds of organizations just represent one great big family. The employers have built themselves up into the hearts of people in the home where the man works. Then, taking a personal interest in one's private problems is a powerful motive for gaining friendly cooperation by helping people solve problems, the people you're associated with, or the people you're working with, and help them solve their problems A lot of people just say, "Oh, well, my problems are mine, and other people's problems are theirs, and I'm not interested in them." You have a right to do that if you want, but that won't be profitable for you.

It won't be beneficial for you, because if you want to have a lot of friends and a lot of cooperation, you'll make it your business to look around and see wherever you can be of help to other people, then you'll start being of help to them.

Many organizations establish a system of friendly competition between departments and in departments between individuals.

In a sales organization, for instance, you can have a different group competing with other different groups in the same organization on a friendly basis, and they'll all strive to do their very best in order to win, because of good sportsmanship.

Able sales managers very often set up that kind of a motive to inspire their sales people to do better jobs. Then, hope of future benefits in the form of some yet unattained goal, which can be attained by mutual cooperation or something that you want to accomplish with a group of people where it can all be accomplished where you are all pulling together in the same direction at the same time in a spirit of perfect harmony.

Maybe in your particular case, you need the cooperation of somebody, and you know what kind of motive you can plant in the mind of that person. You can't get it by force or coercion and hope to benefit by that method, because if you get it by that method, sooner or later, the cooperation will play out and turn into resentment.

Andrew Carnegie's method of inspiring cooperation was based on a monetary motive through promotions and bonuses. That was one of his most potent and most influential motives for getting people to cooperate.

All the people who worked for Andrew Carnegie knew they had the potential possibility of becoming an exceedingly well-paid executive. These people had seen individual after individual do that very thing by starting low in the ranks and climbing right up to the top.

In his question system, he never reprimanded any employee offensively and allowed the employee who deserved it to reprimand themselves through carefully directed questions. When Mr. Carnegie wanted to reprimand a person or discipline them, he would call them into his office and start asking them questions. He would ask questions the way Mr. Carnegie wanted them answered, and I think that was very smart.

If Mr. Carnegie wanted the fault brought out, he'd let the person bring out the fault, because he'd put questions to them that would force them to bring out the fault or tell a lie. Of course, they didn't want to do that, especially when they knew Mr. Carnegie knew what the lie was. That was one of the things that indicated what a smart man Mr. Carnegie was, because he always got the best results out of individuals without unnecessarily hurting them or offending them.

Mr. Carnegie always had one or more people in

training for his job, and several of them made it. Isn't that a great thing for an employer to have a number of people standing around training for his job? You don't think they would be disloyal or lay down on the job or refuse to go the extra mile, do you? They would be silly if they did. Mr. Carnegie knew how to hang out plums for people to reach for, and while he kept that plum just a little bit ahead of the reach of the person, he caused them to grow a stronger and longer arm for reaching.

That was much better than throwing the fear into a man's heart of losing his job, as so many employers have done. He never made decisions for his employees, but always encouraged them to make their own decisions and be responsible for the results thereof. Mr. Carnegie would not make decisions for his executives, for his under-executives, and for those who were in training for executive jobs.

That's one thing that made Mr. Carnegie such a successful man. He taught individuals to not only make decisions, but also be responsible for the decisions when they made them. That's an important little item, too. Our American system of free enterprise gets friendly cooperation when it is not interfered with by outside influences by the profit motive.

In the United States, if we took away the profit motive, it would take away the very warp and woof of our whole system of free enterprise. We have one of the finest combinations of motives that exist anywhere in the world.

I don't know what you think about this philosophy as far as you may have gone. I just want you to know if you can just get 50 percent of the benefits that are available to you out of this philosophy, you can so thoroughly change your life. The next coming year ahead of you can be the most outstanding year of your life, and from here on out, you can enjoy a controlled destiny, one you'll hew out for yourself and where you'll find happiness, pleasure, contentment, security, and where you will enjoy the friendship and goodwill of the people around you, because you will create the circumstances leading to that end.

Is there not food for thought in the fact that no newspaper has ever published any account of wild drinking parties or other similar scandals in connection with names such as Edison, Ford, Rockefeller, and most of the other really big fellows?

14

CREATIVE VISION OR IMAGINATION

The imagination of someone is the workshop wherein we fashion the purpose of the brain and the ideas of the soul. You will not find a better definition than that one. Basically, new things are few and far between. As a matter of fact, when you speak of somebody creating a new idea or anything new, the chances are one thousand to one it's not anything actually new. It's a reassembling of something that's old and something that's gone before.

The creative imagination operating through the sixth sense in the subconscious mind has its base in the subconscious section of the brain and serves as the medium by which basically new facts or ideas are revealed. Any idea, plan, or purpose brought into the conscious mind and repeated and supported by emotional feelings is automatically picked up by the subconscious section of the brain and carried out to its logical conclusion by whatever natural and logical means that are practical and convenient. These ideas you have in your mind that you're not emotionalized over or in which you're not enthusiastic about or in which you don't have applied faith seldom produce any action.

You've got to get emotion into your thoughts, and you got to have enthusiasm in your thoughts and have applied faith to get any action.

There are two forms of imagination. The first one is synthetic imagination, which consists of a combination of recognized old ideas, concepts, plans or facts arranged in a new combination. Mr. Edison's invention of the incandescent electric light bulb is an example of synthetic imagination applied: You may be interested in knowing there was nothing new about Edison's electric light bulb.

Both of the factors when combined that made up the incandescent electric light bulb were old and well-known to the world long before Edison's time. It remained for Thomas A. Edison to go through ten thousand different failures and find a way of marrying these two old ideas and bringing them together in a new combination.

One of the ideas was based on the fact you could take and apply electrical energy to a wire, and at the point of friction the wire would become hot, and then would make a light.

A lot of people found that out before Edison's time, but Mr. Edison's problem was in finding some means of controlling that wire so when it was heated to a white heat to make light it wouldn't burn up.

Mr. Edison tried all those experiments, to be exact, over ten thousand of them, and none of them worked. Then one day, as was his custom, he laid down for one of those catnaps to turn the problem over to his subconscious mind.

While he was asleep, the subconscious mind came up with the answer. Mr. Edison woke up after one of those catnaps, came out of his sleep, and saw the solution to the other half of his idea. He had half of his idea already, but he saw the solution to the other half of his problem. It consisted of the charcoal principle.

To produce charcoal, you put a pile of wood on the ground and set it on fire. You cover the wood with just enough dirt allowing just enough oxygen to percolate through to keep the wood smoldering, but not enough to permit it to blaze.

It burns away a certain part of the wood, leaving the rest, which is called charcoal. You know where there is no oxygen, there can be no combustion.

Taking that concept with which Mr. Edison had long been familiar, he went back into his laboratory and took the wire that he had been heating with electricity. He put the wire into a bottle, pumped all the air out of the bottle, and sealed the bottle, cutting off all oxygen. No oxygen could come into contact with the wire. Then he turned on the electrical power, and it burned for eight and a half hours. That's the principle to this very day under which the electric lamp operates. That's why when you drop one of those bulbs it pops like a gun. All the air had been drawn out of the bulb.

The reason being you cannot permit any oxygen to be inside of the bulb. If the oxygen were there, it would have quickly burned up the filament. Here were two old simple ideas brought together through synthetic imagination.

If you'll examine the operations of your imagination, or the imaginations of successful people, you will find in a large proportion of cases what has been used is synthetic imagination and not creative imagination. These ideas of giving rearrangement to old ideas and old concepts can be very profitable.

You may have discovered there is nothing new in this philosophy you're reading. Everything is as old as mankind. What did I do? I used my synthetic imagination, reassembled, and sorted out the salient things that go into the making of success. I organized them in the way they had never been organized before in the history of the world, organized them in a simple book form where you or anyone else can take a hold of them and put them to practical use.

I wonder why somebody smarter than me hasn't done this before now.

When we get hold of a good idea, we are always inclined to go back and say, "I wonder why I didn't think of that." If you get it, you will say, "Why in the world didn't I think of that a long time ago when I was needing the money?"

Henry Ford's combination of the horse-drawn buggy and steam-propelled threshing machine is nothing in the world but the use of synthetic imagination. He was inspired to create the automobile when he saw his first threshing machine outfit being pulled along by a steam-propelled engine.

Mr. Ford observed it, and then and there, he got the idea of taking that same principle, putting it onto a buggy instead of the horse, making the horseless buggy, which eventually turned out to be known as the automobile.

Basically, all new ideas originate through single or mastermind application of creative vision and generally, through the mastermind application of creative vision.

You'll observe when two or more people get together and begin to think along the same line in the spirit of perfect harmony, then work up enthusiasm, all the people in the group begin to get ideas. Out of the group someone will come up with an idea pertaining to the thing they are discussing in the main.

If the group goes into a discussion for the solution of a major problem, somebody will find the answer, depending on whose subconscious mind tunes into the infinite storehouse and picks the answer out first. Oftentimes, the answer will not come from the smartest or most brilliant or best-educated person in the group. Oftentimes, it will come from the least educated and the least brilliant person in the group.

Here are some examples of creative imagination:

Take radium, discovered by Madame Curie, and all Madame Curie knew was theoretically there should be some radium somewhere in the universe. She hoped it would be on this little ball of mud we call the earth. She had a definite major purpose, had a definite idea, worked it out mathematically, and determined there was radium somewhere available, even though nobody had ever seen, produced, or refined any.

Imagine Madame Curie starting out to find radium in comparison with the proverbial story about the person looking for a needle in a haystack. Do you have any idea what gave her the first cues and how she went about searching for it? You don't think for a moment she went out with a spade and a shovel digging in the ground looking for it? Oh, no, she wasn't that foolish; she conditioned her mind to tune in on infinite intelligence, and infinite intelligence directed her to the source, the exact process you use in attracting riches or attracting anything else you want.

You must first condition your mind with a definite picture of the thing you want, build it up, and support it with faith in your belief that you're going to get the thing you want most, and you keep on wanting it, even if the going gets hard.

Radar and the radio are both products of creative imagination. The Wright brothers' flying machine is a product of creative imagination. Nobody had ever created and successfully flown a heavier-than-air machine until the Wright brothers produced theirs.

The Wright brothers had no encouragement from the public, and announced they had flown it successfully and wanted to demonstrate it again down at Kitty Hawk, North Carolina. When it was announced to the press, the newspapermen were so skeptical not one single solitary newspaperman went down there on the biggest scoop in the last one hundred years.

How many people do we see like that all the way through life? These smart alecks, these wise guys, and these people who don't believe it can done, because it has never been done before in the history of the world. There is no limitation to the application of creative vision. The person who can condition their mind to tune in on infinite intelligence can come up with the answer to anything that has an answer, no matter how difficult the problem.

Mr. Edison created one idea I know about that came out of creative vision. It was the talking machine, and before Mr. Edison's time, nobody had ever recorded or reproduced sound of any kind or anything even resembling it. Mr. Edison conceived that idea, and almost instantaneously took a piece of paper out of his pocket, and with a pencil drew a crude sketch of what later became known as the first

Edison talking machine, one that had a cylinder on it. When they tried the model out, the thing worked the very first time. You see, the law of compensation had paid him off for those ten thousand failures while he was working out the incandescent electric lamp. Don't you see how fair and generous the law of compensation is? Where you seem to be cheated in one place, it will be made up in some other place in proportion to your desserts, whatever your desserts may be.

That works with penalizing, too, because when you escape the cop at one corner where you ran a red light, maybe you will escape him again, but next time he'll catch you on two or three counts.

Well, off here in nature somewhere there's a tremendous cop and a tremendous recording machine that records all our good qualities and all our bad ones, all our mistakes, and all our successes, and sooner or later they all catch up with us.

With creative vision in evaluating the great American way of life, we still enjoy the privilege of freedom. We have the richest and freest country ever known to mankind. We need to use vision if we are to continue to enjoy these great blessings. If you will look backward and see what traits of character have made our country great, you will find the leaders who have been responsible for what we have in the American way of life.

They made definite application of the seventeen

principles of the philosophy of American achievement with emphasis on six of them. At that time these principles were not called by these names, and many of the great men and women using them weren't conscious they were applying these principles.

One of the strangest facts about all the successful men Mr. Hill had interviewed and worked with was not one single solitary one of them could sit down and categorically give him a step-by-step modus operandi by which they had succeeded. These men had stumbled upon these principles, mind you, by sheer accident.

I want you to go back and measure the fifty-six men who signed the Declaration of Independence.

I want you to go back and measure what these men did by these six principles. Then, you can definitely trace them to the application of their act.

- A definite major purpose
- Going the extra mile
- The mastermind principle
- Creative vision
- Applied faith
- Personal initiative

The makers of the American way of life did not expect something for nothing.

The makers of the American way of life did not regulate their working hours with the time clock.

The makers of the American way of life assumed full responsibilities of leadership even when the going was hard.

As we look backward over the past one hundred years of creative vision, we find Thomas A. Edison, through his creative vision and personal initiative, ushering in the great electrical age, which gave us a source of power the world would not previously know. That one man ushered in the great electrical age, without which all the industrial improvements we had, like radar, television, and radio, would not be possible or even in existence. What a great thing Mr. Edison did to influence the trend of civilization all over the world!

What a great thing Mr. Ford did when he brought in the automobile. Mr. Ford brought backwoods and main streets together. Mr. Ford shortened distances and improved the values of lands by causing marvelous roads to be built through them. He gave employment directly and indirectly to millions of people who today have businesses supplying the automobile trade.

Wilbur and Orville Wright changed the size of the earth, so to speak, and shortened distances all over the world just by those two great men operating for the good of mankind.

Andrew Carnegie, through his creative vision and personal initiative, ushered in the great steel age, which revolutionized our entire industrial system and made possible the birth of myriad industries, which could not have existed without steel.

Not satisfied with the accumulation of a vast fortune of his own and raising of scores of his associate workers into sizeable fortunes they could not have accumulated without Andrew Carnegie's aid.

Mr. Carnegie finished his life by inspiring the organization of the world's first practical philosophy of American achievement, which makes the know-how of success available to the humblest person.

When you begin to analyze what's happened here and what a great thing can take place when an individual gets together with another individual and forms a mastermind alliance and begins to do something useful for his country.

Without my mastermind alliance, if I had a thousand lives to live, I could have never written this book.

The inspiration, the faith, the confidence, and the go-ahead spirit I got from having access to Napoleon Hill's books and lectures enabled me to rise to his level.

I could have never done without this mastermind principle and without creative vision.

There were many times in my life when logically if I had listened to what seemed logical and reasonable, would have quit trying to complete this book and gone back to work as a prison guard as my former wife said she thought I should have done. I would be making $75,000 per year, been very secure, and everything would have been lovely in my life.

I did fight that successfully. I saw bigger things. I began to not only use my synthetic imagination, but also my creative imagination, and particularly, my creative vision.

That enabled me to pull aside the curtain of discouragement and despair, and look into the future to see what's taking place all over the world as a result of my having passed this way. All of that was through creative vision, and what a great thing it is to be able to tap into that thing called creative vision, and through it to tune in to the powers of the universe.

I'm not making a poetic speech. I'm citing science, and it can be done by you, too.

Here is a bird's-eye view of what men and women with creative vision and personal initiative have given our great country. First, it was the automobile, which has changed our entire way of living today. The whole method of transportation has changed, and the whole method of doing business has changed as a result of that one thing called the automobile.

Then we have airplanes which travel faster than sound and have shrunk the world to where people of all countries know one another better. Perhaps the Creator intended it that way instead of all these wars and these things that we've been having in the past.

If we reduced the world in size and brought people of all nations together within a travel distance of twenty-four hours.

We would all become better acquainted, all become neighbors, and finally, all become brothers and sisters under the skin as well as on the skin. When the brotherhood of man takes place, it will be because of these various marvelous things the imagination of man has uncovered and has revealed that brings us much closer together, making it more convenient for us to assemble and understand each other all over the world. You can't carry on a war with the person you're doing business with or the neighbor you live by each day and have peace of mind.

We must manage to get along with people we come into contact with every day.

Also, we have radio and television which give us the news of the world almost as fast as it happens. They provide us with the finest entertainment from log cabins in mountain country and city mansions alike. That's quite an advancement over the days of Lincoln as he learned to write on the back of a wooden shovel in a one-room log cabin.

Today you can push a remote control and tune in to the finest operas, the finest music, and the finest everything, and know what the world is doing almost as fast as it's happening. Throughout the whole world you can see the results of what man's mind has brought forth to introduce people to one another.

John West

*Some men die too soon from overeating,
others die from strong drink, while others just
wither up and die because they have nothing to do.*

15

THE MAINTENANCE OF SOUND HEALTH

I have a pretty good system for keeping myself healthy and full of energy, If I didn't I couldn't have done the necessary research and the amount of work that I've done in years past.

I couldn't do the amount of work that I'm doing today, at my age and the condition I'm in.

I can run rings around people half my age who don't have the system I have.

I have to keep myself in that condition and there are several reasons for keeping myself in that condition.

I enjoy living better if my body responds because I don't want to get up in the morning ailing.

I hope you can get some good suggestions out of this chapter to help keep your physical body stay in fine condition all the time.

Let's take up a positive mental attitude.

A positive mental attitude should come at the top of your list because without a positive health consciousness or thinking and acting in terms of health, the chances are you're not going to be healthy.

I never think of ailments.

I can't afford ailments because they take up too much of my time, and they disturb my mental attitude.

How does one keep from having any ailments because I have them did I hear you say?

There should be no griping in family and occupational relationships because it hurts the digestion.

You might say, "Well, I have certain circumstances in my family that makes it necessary for me to gripe and to complain."

Alright, change the circumstances so you don't have any circumstances for griping and complaining.

The reason I mention family and occupational relationships is because there is where you spend most of your life. If you're going to allow these relationships to be based upon friction and upon misunderstandings and upon arguments.

Then you're not going to have good health and you're not going to be happy and you're not going to have peace of mind.

There should be no hatred no matter how much a person deserves to be hated.

It produces stomach ulcers.

It produces a negative mental attitude that repels

people from you instead of attracting them to you.

If you hate people, they will hate you.

They may not say so, but they will hate you if you hate them.

There should be no gossip or slander because it hurts the digestion.

That's a very hard one to comply with today because there's so much wonderful material to gossip about in the world.

Let's transmute that desire to gossip into something that's much more profitable for you.

Because slander and gossip attract reprisals and it also hurts the digestion, there should be no fear because that indicates friction in human relationships and hurts the digestion.

I can truthfully say there isn't anything on the face of this earth or in the universe I survey around me I fear.

I'd have it out with myself and eliminate the cause of that fear no matter what it took or how long it took.

I will not tolerate fear in my makeup because you can't have good health, you can't be prosperous, and you can't be happy or have peace of mind if you're going to fear anything, even death.

I'm looking forward to death. It's going to be one of the most unusual interludes of my entire life.

It's going to be the last thing I do and the most wonderful things of all because I'm not afraid of dying.

There should be no envy, because it indicates lack of self-reliance, and it also hurts the digestion.

There are six things that I will give you in the way of do's that will enable you to maintain a positive mental attitude that is conducive to a health consciousness.

Did you know the way you use your mind has more to do with your health than from all other things combined?

You can talk about germs getting into the blood all you want. Nature has set up a great system of doctoring inside of you, and germ or no germ, if that system is working properly, the resistance in your physical body will take care of all those germs.

Mother Nature has a way of keeping down through body resistance the supply so those germs cannot multiply.

The very minute you become worried or annoyed or afraid and you break down that body resistance.

Those germs begin to multiply by the billions and trillions and quadrillions and then you really are sick.

Eating Habits

You can learn to prepare your mind to aid you while eating with peace of mind.

The best way to do it is there should be no worries

or arguments or unpleasantness at mealtime.

Did you know the average family selects mealtime for the time to discipline children or to discipline the wife and children, as the case may be?

That's one time when you can get them all together and when they're not inclined to run away and then you can give them a tongue-lashing.

They will sit it out and eat while you're saying your peace but, if you could see what happens to the digestion and to the bloodstream.

A kid who eats while they're undergoing punishment is the wrong time to discipline a child.

The thoughts you have while you're eating go into the food you eat and become a part of the energy that goes into the bloodstream.

Then, with overeating all it does is overworks the heart, the lungs, the liver, the kidneys, and the sewer system.

Most people eat twice as much as they really could get along with daily.

Just think of the amount of money you'd save nowadays with the cost of groceries as high as they are in grocery stores.

It's astounding how much people overeat, like the ones who are doing secretary occupations or work inside a building.

A man digging ditches has to have a certain amount

of meat and potatoes or something that's equal.

A person doing office work or in a store or in a house doesn't have to have the same amount of heavy, substantial food that he or she would need doing heavy manual labor in their life.

You can eat a balanced ration with fruits and vegetables and plenty of water or the equivalent of water, in the form of juices.

You shouldn't eat too rapidly because it prevents proper mastication.

There are a lot of people who eat too rapidly and that shows you have got too much on your mind.

A meal should be a form of worship with your beautiful thoughts on all the beautiful things you want to do, like your definite major purpose and the things that please you the most while you're eating.

If you're eating with someone else or engaged in conversation while eating, the conversation should be a pleasant conversation not a faultfinding or fishing job.

A man sitting across from the table of a beautiful woman should talk about her beautiful eyes, and her hairdo, and her lipstick, all the things pretty women likes you to talk about if you're the right man.

If you're sitting across the table from your wife, I don't know any reason in the world why it wouldn't help you and her, too.

You shouldn't eat very many candy bars or peanuts or snacks or drink too many soft drinks between meals.

I know some office girls that make a whole lunch off candy bars and knick-knacks and a bottle or two of soda pop from the Coke machine.

A young person's stomach can stand that for a while, but if your stomach is not being treated properly, sooner or later nature will make you pay up for that kind of mistreatment of your stomach.

It would be far better if an office worker would go out and get a head of lettuce and put on it some salad dressing.

Maybe get some fruit or some grapes or anything else you can get at the fruit stand, especially if you live in California.

Liquor in excess is taboo at all times, except after a wedding. That was meant to be funny.

I don't mean exactly what I said, but if it is in "excess," then, yes, I would say it is taboo at all times.

Liquor in reasonable amounts I don't think is too bad.

I can take a cocktail or two and that would about be my limit at one time.

I could take three on occasion I suppose and then I'd commence to say some of the things maybe I ought not to say then do some of the things I ought not to do and it wouldn't do me any good.

What's the sense of tickling your stomach and your brain so you're not yourself?

People find out too much stuff about you that you don't want them to know about you.

Don't you think a person whose tongue has been loosened up with liquor make a spectacle out of themselves at these fun parties?

If I go into a home where they have cocktails, I don't say, "Oh, no, I don't touch the stuff."

I can take a cocktail and if I'm not in the mood to drink I set it down somewhere or when no one is looking I dump it into the sink.

Then with any bad habits like liquor or smoking if it's moderate and you take it instead of it taking you then I would say it wouldn't be too bad for you.

Of course, the better overall plan is to get over using these poisons.

Relaxation

You need play to ensure sound health, therefore, you should balance all work with an equivalent amount of play. That doesn't always mean an equivalent number of hours because sometimes it just doesn't work out that way.

I can work one hour and within twenty minutes of playing I can offset my work.

I'm an inspirational writer as you may have guessed.

I write when I'm all keyed up on another plane.

If it's intense, then I go for a nice little walk and get outside and get some fresh air.

Then I've completely balanced off the intense activity I have been engaged in.

Then sleep eight hours out of every twenty-four if you can find some time to get some good sleep.

When I say sleep, I mean get in that bed and lie down and don't turn and twist and groan and snore and all that sort of things.

Get in such good rapport with yourself and with your own conscience and with all your neighbors you don't have anything to worry about.

Train yourself not to worry over things you can't remedy. It's bad enough for you to worry over the things you can remedy.

There are a lot of people in the world who not only make room in their own life for all of their own problems, These people take on the problems of all their in-laws and all their relatives and all their friends and all the problems of the whole neighborhood.

Sometimes all the problems of the whole nation.

You shouldn't look for trouble.

It will find you in its own way too soon because the circumstances of life have a queer way of revealing to you the thing you're searching for in life.

You don't even have to go out of your own house to find a lot of things to worry about if you're looking for things to worry about outside of your house.

Hope

Hope inspires sound health and sound health inspires hope. I mean, hope of some yet-unattained objective you're working toward and something you're going to do it within the time you set for your goal.

There are many people in the world who start out to be rich.

They want to make a lot of money and get impatient and become nervous and work themselves into a fury because they don't get the money fast enough.

Sometimes the desire to get money quickly influences people to get it the wrong way.

Develop hope by daily prayer not for more blessings but for those you already have, such as freedom as an American citizen.

What a great thing it would be if you express a prayer every day, in your own words, or you don't need to use any words.

In your own thoughts, express a prayer for the appreciation of the freedom you enjoy as an American citizen, the freedom to be ourselves and the freedom to live our own lives in our own way.

The freedom we have to have our own objectives.

Then the freedom to make our own friends.

To vote as we please and worship as we please and to do pretty much anything else that we desire or please.

Economic Freedom

Let's take a look at the opportunity you have to secure economic freedom according to your talents.

Take the opportunity to give gratitude for the freedom you have to worship in your own way with sound physical and mental sound health.

Then the opportunity to give gratitude of all the great things that still exist in the time still ahead of you.

The richest part of my life and of my achievements is just beginning.

I'm just a youngster in the business and I have been going through kindergarten.

You should clean out your medicine chest and throwaway all of those aspirin and headache tablets.

Headache is nothing in the world but Mother Nature telling you there's some trouble somewhere and you'd better get busy and do something about it and fix the problem.

Did you know that physical pain is one of the most miraculous and most marvelous things of all of nature's creations?

It's the only universal language that every living creature begins to do something about it when physical pain begins to clamp down on him or her because it is a form of warning.

Remember, sound health does not come from bottles.

It comes from fresh air, wholesome food, and wholesome thinking and living habits, all of which is under our control.

Work

Work must be a blessing because God provided every living creature must engage in it in one way or another or perish.

Talk about the birds of the air and the beasts of the jungle, neither spinning nor sewing nor reaping but nevertheless they have to work before they can eat.

Work should be performed in the spirit of worship as a ceremony.

Did you know when you're engaged in a labor of love and you're doing something for somebody just because you love that person or he or she is a friend of yours.

You never feel tired when you're doing that kind of work.

Work should be based on the hope of achievement of some definite major purpose.

Thus, it becomes voluntary, a pleasure to be sought and not a burden to be endured.

You can learn to work in a spirit of gratitude for the blessings work provides in both sound physical and mental health.

Having economic security helps one provide for their dependents, thus it should embellished with love.

Faith

You can learn to communicate with infinite intelligence from within and adapt yourself to the laws of nature as they are in evidence all around us.

One of the greatest systems of therapeutics I know anything about is an abiding and enduring source of faith.

If by chance legitimate ailments do happen to creep in, I don't know of any other better medicine to take than faith.

All anyone really requires as capital on which to start a successful career is a sound mind, a healthy body, and a genuine desire to be of as much service as possible to as many people as possible.

16

BUDGETING TIME AND MONEY

If you want to have financial security in this world, you've got to do two things.

You've got to make the best use of your time and you will have to budget expenditures and your receipts.

We have twenty-four hours and you can divide those into three eight-hour periods.

We have eight hours for sleep and another eight hours for work.

We don't always have too much control over the eight hours we put in for sleep.

Those have to be given over to nature and she demands those eight hours.

You don't always have too much control over the eight hours you put into your work.

If you're working for yourself, you still you have to be on the job.

Then we have another eight hours of extra time and bless your life you can waste them if you want to waste them. You can play or you can work or you can enjoy yourself and relax or you can develop by taking courses of instruction.

You can read books or listen to motivational tapes or do anything you want with all that extra time.

It used to be while I was doing my research I worked sixteen hours a day.

It was a labor of love I was engaged in.

I reserved eight hours a day for sleep and the other sixteen I worked.

Part of the time, in order to make a living but mostly in research to complete this book and give it to the world.

If it had not been for the fact I had at least eight hours of free time I never could have done the necessary research for this book.

In the eight hours of your spare time, you can practice developing good habits and you don't have to follow my plan.

You can get some mighty good ideas in the chapter on applied faith and the chapter on the mastermind and the chapter on the law of cosmic habit force.

You can work out a plan of your own because it would be better for you then if I give it to you to follow.

Budgeting of income and expenses should be first on your list.

You can put down a monthly or weekly amount of your income and keep a regular budgeting book.

If you have a family or you don't have a family, a life insurance policy is an absolute must because you just cannot afford to be without one.

If you brought children into this world it's your responsibility for their education.

It's up to you to insure yourself so if you should pass out of the picture they have enough money to educate themselves if something happened.

If you've married and have a wife who's entirely dependent upon you.

It's up to you to carry enough insurance to give her a down payment on a second husband if you should pass out of the picture.

Life insurance gives you such great protection in case you are taken away from your source of production.

A key person in a business or has a family where their services are a large portion of the assets.

These people should always be insured for a large enough sum of money to fill up the chasm in case something happens and they're taken out of the picture.

You can put aside a definite percentage of your income for food, clothing, and housing.

Don't just go out and blow the works.

You can go out to the grocery store and always spend five times much more then you actually need.

I do the shopping at my house, that way I can get what I want to eat.

I've learned a great deal about shopping by following around those housewives who are good shoppers and start asking them questions about buying and handling food.

They put me onto a lot of things I didn't know about buying food.

Especially, about handling food after I buy it and putting it into the freezer.

When I go to one of those big supermarkets.

I always pick out the most likely housewife.

I follow along behind one and start asking her questions.

They just love to tell me what I should and shouldn't do.

You can set aside a definite amount for investments, even if it's only a small amount, like a dollar a week, even fifty cents a week.

It's not the amount you set aside, it's the habit of being resourceful and frugal.

I've always admired someone who doesn't waste things. There was this old man in my hometown and he would ride his bike around town picking up old nails and strings and pieces of metal and put it in a basket on the handle bar of his bike.

My frugality never ran into that extent in my life.

It ran more into BMW's and half million-dollar estates.

Believe me, I got around at long last learning that no matter how much of this philosophy you have.

If you don't have a system for saving a part that goes through your hands.

It makes no difference, and it will all go through.

Then whatever amount remains after you have taken care of those three items should go into a current checking or spending account for emergencies, recreation, education, etc.

You can draw on that and you don't have to follow your budget on that plan.

You can say that's a petty cash account.

If you're real frugal, you let it get up to a pretty good size and not keep it down too low all the time.

When you have a good nest egg lying in the bank or in your savings account, no matter what happens you can go down to the bank to get some money.

You might not need it and the chances are it will put you in that frame of mind where you won't have to go down to the bank and get it.

If you don't have it there you will have a million needs and you will be afraid with all of them.

I think perhaps what gives me the most courage to speak my piece and be myself and demand people keep off of my toes.

It's the fact I no longer have to worry where my money is coming from.

There are some people who try to worry me, but it's like Confucius said, when rat tries to pull cat's whiskers, rat generally winds up in honorable cat's belly.

You can keep a system of tracking the percentage that goes through your hands and establish a frugal savings habit.

If your income is too low you can't cut anymore out of your expenses try taking off the top 1 percent out of every dollar. Take 1 percent off and put it away someplace where it's hard for you to get it so you won't spend it.

I'm a great believer in having money invested in investment trusts.

The ones where they represent a great variety of well-known stocks.

There are a some of those investment trusts that are good and some not so good.

If you go to invest in an investment trust, you should go to your banker or Charles Schwab or somebody who's acquainted in investment trusts.

An individual is usually not qualified doing it own their own judgment.

Try to get some of your money working for you.

You will be surprised at what a nice gain you get.

When you know your setting aside a certain amount every month or even every week, it gives you peace of mind.

I mean get it someplace where you can't reach down in your pocket and get it out then spend all your money.

When every so often go to the bank to get pocket money.

I always take a $20 bill and put it in that little special pocket in my wallet.

If I happen to run out of money, I'll always have $20. Saving money becomes very difficult for most people because most people don't have any system to go by in their life.

Choice of Occupation

Have you given any thought of getting yourself adjusted in an occupation or a business or a profession that can be a labor of love in your life?

Business and Personal Relationships

Are you putting in some of your time with personal relationships or good will building in your relationships with other people?

If you don't, you're not going to have any friends because out of sight out of mind.

I don't care how good the friend is, if you don't keep in contact with them, they'll forget about you ever existing.

Religion

Then with your religion are you putting in some time living your religion?

I'm not talking about going to church and throwing a nickel in the basket, because anybody can do that as a regular thing.

Are you living your religion in your bedroom and in your drawing room and in your kitchen and in your place of business or your office?

Chances are, you go to church once a week, maybe more, because some religions you have to go more.

It's not how many times you go that count.

It's not how much you contribute to the church in the way of money.

It's what you do to live that religion in everyday ways of living.

You know all of the religions of the world would be wonderful if people would only live by them instead of just believing in them.

I don't know of any religion on the face of this earth that wouldn't be wonderful if people would only live by them.

Use of Your Spare Time

With the eight hours of your spare time are you devoting it to some sort of advancement of your interests or the improvement of your mind or benefiting by association?

How much o time do you spend developing a budgeting system for the spending of your money?

There may be some weeks you may have to cheat a little bit.

You can always pay it back the next week when you don't have to cheat.

Are you spending some time studying the chapter on accurate thinking?

Are you putting in some time actually learning how to think accurately?

Are you controlling your thoughts or are your thoughts uncontrolled?

Are you letting the circumstances of life control you or are you trying to create the circumstances you can control? You can't control all of them, nobody can do that, but you can create some circumstances that you can control.

This privilege of voting, do you say, "Oh well, I guess I'll not go to the polls, the crooks are going to run the country anyway and my little vote's not going to count"?

Do you say that, or do you say, "I have a responsibility and I'm going to go to the polls and vote because that's my duty to put the right people in office."

There are too many people who don't and that's why there are so many crooked politicians and others in public office that shouldn't be in office.

It's because there are too many decent people don't vote.

Then your family relationships, are they harmonious and do you have a mastermind relationship?

If the wife won't give in, why don't you give in or vice versa?

You made it interesting for each other before you each married each other or you wouldn't have got married.

Why don't you try it all over again and renegotiate your marriage relationship, so you will have a wonderful relationship in your family?

It will pay off in peace of mind and will pay off in dollars and cents.

It will pay off in friendships and it will pay off in every which way you want to judge it.

In your job or your profession, are you going the extra mile and do you like your work?

In what ways are you going the extra mile? Are you going the extra mile in the right sort of positive mental attitude?

The Habits of Thought

How much of your time are you putting in on the can-do sort of thinking and not the no-can-do part of thinking? Have you ever stopped and sat down and took inventory to see how much of your time goes to the things you don't desire?

Things like fear and ill health and frustrations and disappointments and discouragements?

You'd be surprised if you had a stopwatch to record the amount of your time you put into every day worrying about things that might happen to you but never do happen.

You should have a budgeting system whereby you keep your mind definitely fixed on the things you do want.

I have a couple hours a day set aside for silent meditation expressing gratitude for the great opportunity I have had to be of service to other people through this book.

If I don't get it in at night, I get it in sometime during the day.

Do you know one of the finest prayers on the face of this earth is not to pray for something but to give gratitude for what you already have?

You have so many riches and you have great health and you live in a wonderful county.

You have wonderful neighbors and you're reading a wonderful book.

Just think of the things you have to be thankful for in the world. Just think of all the things I have to be thankful for. It's no wonder I'm rich.

I can be the master of my fate and the captain of my soul because I live by my philosophy.

It's designed to help other people and never under any circumstance do I intentionally hinder or harm or endanger another person.

If you can make it your business to go the extra mile with every person you come into contact with.

The time will come when you will have so many wonderful friends that whatever it is you want them to carry out they will be at your beck and call.

You can search the world over and you'll never find a more wonderful relationship then I have with everyone in the world.

I wanted to earn it and deserve it.

Nobody can have anything in the world worth having without first earning it.

Who told you it couldn't be done? And what great achievement has he to his credit that entitles him to use the word "impossible" so freely?

17

THE LAW OF COSMIC HABIT FORCE

If you are a student of Emerson and read the law of compensation, or you're a student of Dr. Napoleon Hill and you've read the law of cosmic habit force.

You will get the sum and the substance of this chapter much more quickly.

This chapter is called the law of cosmic habit force.

It is the controlling force of all the natural laws of the universe.

We have many natural laws and obviously they all work automatically, and they're not suspended for one moment for anybody.

Those laws are laid down so the individual who makes it his or her business to understand them and adapt themselves to them can go very far in life.

Those who do not understand them and adapt themselves to them go down in defeat.

I want you to recognize an individual has control over but one thing and that's the privilege of forming their own habits.

Individuals can tear them down or replace them with others or refine them or change them and doing anything they want to do with them.

Individuals have that complete privilege.

We are the only creatures on the face of this earth who have that privilege.

Every other living thing below the intelligence of man that comes into life has its life pattern and its destiny fixed and it's called instinct.

I want you to know men and women are not bound by instinct.

Men and women are bound only by their imagination and the willpower of their own mind.

Individuals can form whatever kind of habits they may need to take them toward their objectives.

The purpose of the *"Great Personal Power"* philosophy is designed to enable one to establish thought patterns that lead to financial security, health, and peace of mind necessary for happiness.

In this chapter, I will briefly describe the established law of nature which make all habits permanent to everything except permanent to mankind.

God gave you complete control over your own mind and he gave you a means of making use of that control.

You can project that mind into whatever objective you please.

Cosmic habit force is the means by which one may set the pattern of his or her own mind.

The habits, which are not fixed by cosmic habit force and which are not subject to suspension or to circumvention, are the stars and planets as they are established in their fixed courses.

Isn't that a wonderful thing to contemplate that all of those millions, billions, trillions, and quadrillions of planets and stars out in the heavens all go along according to a system?

Those planets and stars never collide with each other.

They are so precise in the system that astronomers can determine hundreds of years in advance the precise relationship of given stars and planets.

Isn't it a marvelous thing to know all of that is carried on according to a system?

If God had to hang out those stars and planets and watch them every night, He'd be a very busy fellow.

He's not going do that because He has a better system that works better and works automatically.

If you will learn those laws and adapt yourself to them, you can profit by them.

If you do not learn those laws, then probably through ignorance or neglect you will suffer all through your life by not using them.

I do notice the majority of people in the world do

not recognize the law of cosmic habit force.

These people go all the way through life using this marvelous law to bring poverty and ill health and frustration and fear and all of those things people do not want by keeping their minds fixed on those things.

I want you to sincerely know it makes no difference what star you were born under.

It makes no difference what other unfavorable circumstance you may have met with in life.

It makes no difference what happened to you in the past.

If you will follow my instructions, you can get from where you are today to where you want to go and you can get there very easy.

You certainly are not going to succeed unless you do understand the law of cosmic habit force and start building the kind of habits that you need to lead you to where you want to go.

Did you know an individual may create the pattern of their thoughts by repetition of thought on a given subject?

Then the law of cosmic habit force takes over these patterns of thought and makes them permanent.

Physical Health

In connection with your physical health, you may

contribute to the healthful maintenance of your physical body by establishing thought habit patterns.

I couldn't write an inspirational book or drive race-cars if I didn't know when I put my foot on the gas, so to speak. There is going to be some *"Great Personal Power."*

Thinking is the first place to start applying cosmic habit force for the purpose of developing sound health.

Having a positive mind leads to the development of what is known as a health consciousness.

You do know what I mean by having a health consciousness or a prosperity consciousness or any other kind of a consciousness, right?

It's an awareness of a condition where you have the predominating tendency to think about health and not about disease or ailments.

The best way is to form a health consciousness is to look in the mirror a dozen times a day and say, "You healthy man," or "You healthy woman."

Having a positive mind leads to the development of what is known as a health consciousness.

Then cosmic habit force will carry out the thought pattern to its logical conclusion in your life.

Cosmic habit force will readily carry out the picture of an ill health consciousness created by the thought habits of a hypochondriac.

It will carry it out to the extent it will produce the physical and the mental symptom of any disease on which the individual may fix their thought habits through fear.

If you think about certain ailments or think about a certain disease long enough, nature will actually simulate it in your physical body.

You can talk yourself into a headache.

You can talk yourself into a bilious condition.

You can talk yourself into anything if you allow your mind to dwell upon the negative sides of your physical body. So thinking is very important.

Did you know the mental attitude you're in while you're eating as the food is being broken down into liquid form for introduction into the blood stream?

That will determine how the food enters the body in a suitable form for the maintenance of sound health.

If you can get into the habit of blessing your food when you sit down at the table while it goes into your body.

That will go a long way towards keeping your body healthy.

Then with work one's mental attitude becomes a vital ally of the silent repairman who is working on every cell of your physical body while engaged in physical action.

I think one of the tragedies of civilization is the fact

there are so few people in the world at any one time engaged in a labor of love.

I'm hoping and I'm praying before I shall have crossed over on the other side.

I will have made valuable contributions to mankind.

To the end every individual in every occupation may find a labor of love in which to make a living and earn their way.

Let's start thinking in terms of good health, of opulence, of plenty, of fellowship and of brotherhood, instead of stirring up race riots and all of those sorts of things like setting man against man, brother against brother, and nation against nation.

There's plenty in the whole world for everybody, including the squirrels, the animals, and the birds.

The famous Mayo brothers have discovered there are four vitally important factors that must be observed to maintain sound physical health, an equal balancing of thought habits in work, play, love and worship, and when these four things—work, play, love, and worship—are out of kilter and out of balance, almost invariably it results to some form of physical ailment.

Here enters a sound explanation of the major reasons for adopting and following the habit of going the extra mile. This habit not only benefits one economically, but it also enables one to work in a positive mental attitude that leads to sound physical health.

When you're doing something out of a spirit of love to be of help to other people and not out of a selfish desire.

It tends to give you better health and helps you to build up much better health habits.

I have an experience in my home that makes me prouder than anything.

Almost invariably when a person walks into my home for the first time, they begin to look around and make some complimentary statement.

I had an outstanding salesman come by my house not long ago.

When I opened the door he looked into my living room and said, "Oh, what a beautiful place. Well, the word 'beautiful' is not the word I mean, it's the way I feel. The vibrations are good."

I said, "You're getting hot, you're getting up my alley."

My home is charged and recharged constantly with positive vibrations.

Even my little dog Chief has picked that up.

He responds to the vibrations of our home.

He can tell when a person is not in harmony with my home the moment they come knocking on the door.

If he doesn't like a person who is not in harmony with my home, he constantly barks at them.

If he's pleased with the harmonious atmosphere, he'll go over and kiss or lick their hand and sniff them.

If he's not pleased and he finds the person not in harmony, he'll bark at them and make them back away.

I didn't teach him that; it was his own idea.

So, homes, places of business, cities, and streets, all have their own vibrations made up of the dominating thoughts of those that work and go that way.

Economic and Financial Benefits

Let's look at the economic and financial benefits that come out of the law of cosmic habit force.

Through the law of cosmic habit force one can establish a definite major purpose.

Then through the combination of the principles of the philosophy of *"Great Personal Power"*, one may condition their mind and body to hand over to cosmic habit force the exact picture of the financial condition or status he or she wishes to maintain.

Conditioning of the mind will automatically be picked up and carried out to its logical conclusion by an inexorable law of nature, which knows no such reality as failure.

I have taken the great opportunity to study very

successful people and observed none of them do the things they can't do.

Mr. Hill once asked Henry Ford if there was anything he wanted to do he couldn't do?

Mr. Ford said, "Why, no, I don't think about the things I can't do, I think about the things I can do."

Many individuals in the world are not like Mr. Ford.

These people think about the things they can't do and worry about them and consequently they can't do them. They think about the money they don't have and worry about not having money and consequently they don't get the money.

You know money is a peculiar thing.

Somehow or another, money just doesn't follow the person around who doesn't believe he or she has a right to get money.

I don't believe it's the fault of the money.

I think it's in the mind of the person who doubts they can get money.

I do notice that when people start believing they can do things, it starts to change their entire financial condition.

So, the whole purpose of this *"Great Personal Power"* philosophy is to induce you to build up habits of belief in yourself and develop your ability to direct your mind into whatever objective you choose.

If you don't know too much about Mahatma Gandhi, it would be a good idea for you to get a book and read up on his life.

I want you to know the fact that no one has ever been known to become financially independent without having first established a prosperity consciousness.

Just as no one may remain physically well without having first established a health consciousness.

My greatest difficulty was changing my thought habits, forgetting I was born in poverty, illiteracy, and ignorance.

When I would pick up a book and read a book about an outstanding man or see an outstanding man.

I would always feel afraid and feel ashamed.

I finally broke my thought pattern and became an inspirational writer.

It's an achievement to reach out and to influence the lives of millions of people all over the world beneficially. I would say that's an achievement.

The fixations of fear and failure

Did you know each one of us came over to this plane with a marvelous doctoring system?

A chemist who breaks up our food and distributes our food and takes out of it the things that nature needs?

So if we think right, eat right, exercise right, and

live right, this doctor inside us will do everything else automatically.

It's a system that nature gave us for balancing everything that we need to keep our body in fine condition all the time.

The fixation of faith

To make use of the fixation of faith and benefit by the law of cosmic habit force, one must work on the fixation of applied faith.

If you tie to applied faith properly when you reach out and call for the things you need.

These things will be where you thought they should be and will be close at hand.

I want you to start following the habits of thinking positive until cosmic habit force takes up your mental attitude and makes it predominately positive all the time.

The best way to keep from being negative is to start building up positive thought habits.

Then let cosmic habit force take over and make your thoughts predominantly positive.

The negatives that you should avoid making into fixations include poverty, imaginary illness, laziness, and just plain everyday garden-variety laziness Envy, greed, anger, hatred, jealousy, dishonesty, drifting without aim or purpose, irritability of mental attitude in general, vanity, arrogance, cynicism, sadism, and the will to injure others. You can't afford these kind of fixations because it's too expensive.

Here are the positives that you can afford to have and you can't afford not to have them:

A definite major purpose must head the list.

Eat it, sleep it, drink it, and indulge in some act every day of your life leading in the direction of your overall lifelong definite major purpose.

Then with the other principles of this philosophy, such as applied faith, personal initiative, enthusiasm, willingness to go the extra mile, imagination, the traits of a pleasing personality, accurate thinking.

These are the things you can afford to make into fixations so that these principles dominate your mind.

You live by them and you think by them and you act by them.

You relate yourself to other people by them on a daily basis by them.

You will be surprised at how quickly you will solve your problems when they arise.

You will wonder why, instead of worrying over your problem, you didn't just get busy and dissolve it or solve it?

Do you know how a professional man like a dentist or lawyer or doctor or engineer goes about attracting a lot of wonderful patients who are agreeable to get along with, wonderful patients who pay their bills promptly, and all that sort of thing?

It starts with the professional individual, because when the professional's mental attitude becomes right, then the client and patient's mental attitude becomes right.

That happens to a merchant or a man or woman in a job, or in any other occupation.

So if we want to reform people, we don't start with the people, we start with us and get our mental attitude right. We are what we are today because of two forms of heredity. One of them we control outright and one of them we do not control outright at all.

Through physical heredity, we bring into this world a little sum total of all of our ancestors.

If we happen to be born with great brainpower or nice, well-developed or rounded-out bodies, fine.

If we happen to be born with a hunchback or some affliction, there's nothing much a person can do about that. Social heredity consists of all of the influences that enter into our life after we were born, and maybe dating back to the prenatal state, even before we were born.

The things we hear, the things we see, the things we are taught, the things we read about, the legends we are influenced constitute social heredity.

The most important part of what happens to us all the way through life is due to our relationship to social heredity, or what we get out of our environment and how much we control our environment.

On this social heredity thing, it's a good idea for all of us adults to go back and reexamine ourselves about the vital things that we think we believe.

Let's find out just what right we have to believe any of them.

I think my beliefs are supported by good sound evidence, or at least what I believe to be sound evidence.

I didn't arrive at that open-minded state of tolerance overnight.

It's certainly not good for anyone to have a closed mind about anything.

I would like to remind you that you may have had a logical excuse for not having forced life to come through with whatever you asked.

But, now that alibi is obsolete because you are now in the possession of the principles that unlock the door to life's bountiful riches, there is no penalty for using them, but there is a price you must pay of failure if you do not use them.

"If we are related," said the immortal Emerson, "we shall meet."

May I borrow his thought and say, if we are related, we have, through these pages, met.

44132733R00186

Made in the USA
Middletown, DE
03 May 2019